Dartnell's
QUICK QUIZZES
133 Ways to Measure Success

Illustrations by Mark Kseniak

DARTNELL is a publisher serving the world of business with books, manuals, newsletters and bulletins, and training materials for executives, managers, supervisors, salespeople, financial officers, personnel executives, and office employees. Dartnell also produces management and sales training videos and audiocassettes, publishes many useful business forms, and many of its materials and films are available in languages other than English. Dartnell, established in 1917, serves the world's business community. For details, catalogs, and product information write:

THE DARTNELL CORPORATION
4660 N. Ravenswood Avenue
Chicago, IL 60640-4595, U.S.A.
Or phone (800) 621-5463 in U.S. and Canada
www.dartnellcorp.com

TABLE OF CONTENTS

INTRODUCTION

What are the benefits of using quizzes as a training tool? To find out, respond **Yes** or **No** to the following statements.

		Yes	No
1.	Quizzes are effective learning tools	☐	☐
2.	Quizzes can help managers, supervisors, and trainers track and improve performance	☐	☐
3.	Quizzes are a way for employees to evaluate their progress.	☐	☐
4.	Quizzes can be used to review and reinforce training	☐	☐
5.	Quizzes can be used to motivate and inspire employees	☐	☐
6.	Quizzes are fun!	☐	☐

If you answered **Yes** to these statements, you understand the value of having an objective, easy-to-use method to evaluate and motivate your employees.

Training can be expensive and time-consuming, but it is a vitally important component of most jobs today. Typically, it falls to managers, supervisors, and trainers to ensure that employees are effectively trained to do the best job they can. Rating performance, tracking progress, and evaluating employees' needs in a wide variety of jobs is a tall order.

Dartnell makes the monitoring and measuring process easier by providing short, self-explanatory quizzes designed for use by supervisors, managers, and trainers in a workplace setting. The quizzes in this book cover key business performance areas, including communication, customer service, teamwork, sales, telephone skills, self-development and interpersonal skills.

These thought-provoking quizzes present proven techniques specifically designed to help individual employees build productive work relationships, handle conflicts in the workplace, and deal with negative feelings that affect productivity and team or coworker morale.

Experts such as Jim Lundy; Patricia Westheimer; David Cleland; Andrew J. DuBrin, Ph.D.; Jeanne M. Wilson; Murray and Neil Raphel; Barbara Glanz; Richard Gerson; Debra J. MacNeil; Odette Polar; Roger Fritz, Ph.D.; and many others provide advice to your employees on how to improve their productivity and their outlook by finding techniques to make their jobs more interesting or by suggesting ways to overcome obstacles that get in the way of success and career development.

Dartnell's quizzes address issues including performance measurement in a team setting, dealing with angry customers, negotiating and listening skills, meeting customer expectations, balancing work and home life, and much more. The 20 or fewer questions or statements that make up each quiz can be answered yes/no, true/false, or check marks. The quizzes are short and can be used as meeting openers or closers or quick reviews. Because the behaviorally based questions and statements are non threatening, they are a fun way for employees to test how far they've come.

After taking the quizzes, employees can check their responses with the answers provided and rate their knowledge of the subject. The quizzes also include explanations of what test-takers' answers mean and specific suggestions for those who might want to improve their skills based on their scores.

Because these interactive quizzes are short, self-directed, and self-scoring, they enable employees to identify factors that can assist them individually in improving their own performance.

Most importantly, quizzes provide supervisors, managers, and trainers with the tools to enhance training programs, track skills development, reinforce learning, and test retention. Designed to supplement and reinforce your in-house or contract training programs, quizzes provide a mechanism for making sure you get the best return on your training dollars.

Encouraging self-directed development in employees is important because the more involved employees are in their training, the more committed they will be to making it work. Using the quizzes in this book is an excellent way for supervisors, managers, and trainers to facilitate the training experience and keep continuous learning going strong.

CHAPTER 1
COMMUNICATION SKILLS
IT'S BOTH WHAT YOU SAY AND HOW YOU SAY IT

Good words are worth much, and cost little.
— **George Herbert**

If any of your employees think communication skills aren't important, ask them what work-related issues they *don't* talk about, read about, or write about at your company. The answer is obvious. What is not obvious, however, is how *well* your employees, supervisors, and managers communicate with each other, with shareholders and vendors, and, of course, with customers.

Are communications always clear? Are the best communication methods consistently used? Do employees take advantage of technology to get their message across? Take a look around you. Excellent communication skills are required everywhere in your company. How do your employees rate? When team leaders, supervisors, or managers deliver presentations, is the message articulated well? Are their remarks focused, geared to the audience, and conveyed with enthusiasm and commitment? Have them rate their presentation skills by taking the quiz "Speaking in Front of a Group" to test how knowledgeable they are about the public speaking process.

Do your employees know what is the appropriate length, tone, and content of an e-mail message? Are they aware of the degree of security involving electronic transmissions? Use the quiz "Watch Your E-Mail Manners" to help your staff maintain or improve the quality of your electronic communications.

When your employees write letters or memos or prepare written documents, do they make sure the language and writing style are appropriate to those who will be reading the correspondence? Is the message proofread and error-free? The quiz "Put Your Writing Skills to the Test" will give your employees a review of basic writing skills and a reminder of the fine points that endow written correspondences with polish and professionalism.

Poorly written internal communications can result in missed deadlines or incorrectly performed jobs. Unclear external communications can confuse customers and suppliers and present your company in a bad light. Faxes or e-mail messages that are too long go unread, and those that contain proprietary or confidential information can compromise individual employees and create liability for your company. Speeches and presentations that are poorly organized, boring, or unnecessary waste the audience's time and cause listeners to question the speaker's credibility.

The quizzes in the chapter can help you get a handle on how well your employees get your company's message across. Speaking and writing clearly, appropriately, and concisely and listening attentively are critical in a rapidly changing business environment in which instant and global communication are possible.

VERBAL SKILLS START WITH THE BASICS

Verbal communication is extremely important in the workplace, as most of your interactions will take this form. To polish your basic skills, focus on learning to use the verbal skills you already have more effectively. To start, take the following quiz, responding **TRUE** or **FALSE** to each statement:

		TRUE	FALSE
1.	I avoid the use of jargon — especially when dealing with people from outside the team.	☐	☐
2.	I articulate my words distinctly, so as not to run them together or drop off endings.	☐	☐
3.	I forgo tired clichés, such as "read my lips," and express my thoughts in my own words.	☐	☐
4.	I don't use unfamiliar words to intimidate my teammates.	☐	☐
5.	I remain silent when formulating thoughts, rather than using fillers, such as "um" and "you know."	☐	☐
6.	When I speak, I am sensitive to individual differences, such as race, gender, and religion.	☐	☐
7.	I don't draw public attention to teammates' errors in grammar or word choice.	☐	☐
8.	I never use profanity in the workplace — even if I think no one can hear me.	☐	☐
9.	Occasionally, I tape-record myself speaking or ask for my teammates' observations to critique my verbal skills.	☐	☐
10.	I make sure to speak up at least once during every team meeting in order to practice my verbal communication.	☐	☐

WHAT'S YOUR SCORE? Strive for a **TRUE** response to each of the above statements in order to make the best use of your verbal communication skills. Remember, your goal should be communication that *expresses* rather than *impresses*. Use your verbal skills as tools.

A POSITIVE SPIN ON WORDS

You've heard the saying, "It's not always what you say but the way you say it." Inflection, tone of voice, and body language carry a lot of communication weight, along with your choice of words.

"Words should convey the positive and avoid the negative," says Debra J. MacNeill in *Customer Service Excellence* (Business One Irwin). As you work with your employees to improve their communication and customer service skills, train them to:

- Think before they speak;
- Take responsibility to help the customer;
- Offer alternative solutions to a problem.

Rephrase the following negative phrases, adapted from MacNeill's book, to accentuate the positive, show that you are taking responsibility to help the customer, or offer choices. (Possible answers are given at the bottom of the page.)

1. You didn't pick up the right form.

   _____

2. We already shut down that operation today; we can't fill your order.

   _____

3. Only authorized employees are allowed back here.

   _____

4. I don't know.

   _____

5. You didn't sign it.

   _____

TURNING NEGATIVES INTO POSITIVES: (1) Several of these forms are similar. Let me show you where we keep the ones we use for this transaction. (2) The machines in that line are out of service until the morning. Can we substitute another part until then? (3) For your protection, only employees from this department are permitted in the machine-service area. (4) That's a good question. Let me find someone who knows the answer. (5) You completed the form correctly. Now if you'll just sign right here we can process the paperwork for you.

ANSWERS START WITH RIGHT QUESTIONS

There are almost as many wrong questions in meetings as there are wrong answers, according to Marion E. Haynes in *Effective Meeting Skills* (Crisp Publications). In the following test, take each situation and match it with the proper response technique. Some response styles may apply to more than one situation:

SITUATIONS

1. You want to stimulate discussion.
2. You want to cut off discussion.
3. You want to bring a teammate into the discussion.
4. Two team members are engaging in a side conversation.
5. You're not sure how to answer a question.
6. You want to test the level of support for a point of view.
7. Two participants are debating a point, and everyone else is listening.
8. Discussion has been going on for some time, and you're unclear about its progress.

RESPONSES

a. Ask each participant to summarize the other's position.
b. Ask for feedback.
c. Ask the group a general question.
d. Ask an individual a specific question.
e. Ask the group a specific question.
f. Ask an individual a general question.
g. Ask the group for a summary.
h. Ask an individual to summarize the discussion.
i. Direct the question back to the group.
j. None of the above.

THE CORRECT QUESTIONS: According to Haynes, these are the proper response tactics: 1. c; 2. h; 3. f; 4. d; 5. i; 6. e; 7. h; and 8. g. If you chose the correct response for seven or eight situations, you are using questions in an effective way to generate meaningful discussion. Six is average, but a lower score indicates you need to improve in this area. Give your colleagues a chance to take this quiz also. Then discuss all your choices to improve meetings.

BREAKING UP COMMUNICATION BLOCKS

To become a true conversationalist, you need to interpret a person's mood and frame of mind to overcome communication barriers. During every conversation, you must pay close attention to what you say and how you say it.

With regard to the following statements, respond **YES** to those that you think are good methods for breaking down communication obstacles and **NO** to those that aren't:

		YES	NO
1.	Discuss people's expectations to be aware of their goals.	☐	☐
2.	Schedule discussions to avoid interrupting colleagues or customers when they're preoccupied or busy.	☐	☐
3.	Realize that different people will have different views about your ideas.	☐	☐
4.	Be direct and say exactly what you're thinking at the time.	☐	☐
5.	Remind people of all your past accomplishments.	☐	☐
6.	Repeat questions back to people to aid your understanding.	☐	☐
7.	Be truthful with your comments to maintain a reputation of credibility.	☐	☐
8.	Listen empathically to people who want to discuss a negative issue.	☐	☐

TOTAL NUMBER OF YES ANSWERS _____

SCORING: Item Nos. 4 and 5 are not good methods to break down communication obstacles. Here's why:

No. 4: Be wary of saying anything you want, when you want to say it. Customers and colleagues will likely view you as pompous and uncaring — and react by closing their ears.

No. 5: If you're a true pro, your actions will speak much louder than your words. Concentrate on doing a superlative job, and avoid fluffing your feathers. Vanity speaks poorly of a person.

WHAT DO YOU SAY WITHOUT WORDS?

Anytime communication takes place face-to-face, the messages you send are not limited to the words you choose. You also send messages through the way in which you hold your hands and arms, where your eyes rest, and countless other nonverbal cues. To be an effective communicator, then, you need to be as concerned about your body language as you are about your verbal choices. Because body language is an easy behavior to notice in others, but far more difficult to analyze in ourselves, have a trusted colleague answer these questions about your behavior. Then, do the same for him or her:

TRUE FALSE

1. Do you make eye contact when speaking with and listening to others? ☐ ☐

2. When you smile, does the sincerity show in your eyes? ☐ ☐

3. Do you avoid crossing your arms over your chest, which can convey that you are closed off to others' thoughts? ☐ ☐

4. When in a group setting, do you avoid turning your back to colleagues, especially when they speak? ☐ ☐

5. Do you assert your ideas confidently, with eyes facing forward, head up, and shoulders back? ☐ ☐

6. Do you avoid distracting actions, such as tapping your pencil on your desk, when listening to others? ☐ ☐

7. Do you keep your eye contact comfortable by not staring? ☐ ☐

8. Do you nod your head and smile, as appropriate, to encourage others as they talk with you? ☐ ☐

9. Do you avoid pointing at colleagues when speaking, or any other gestures that could seem aggressive? ☐ ☐

10. Does your body language match and thus reinforce what you are saying? ☐ ☐

WHAT'S YOUR SCORE? A score of eight or more **YES** answers indicates that you are using body language that is appropriate to the situation in most cases. As you think more about your nonverbal messages, you'll begin to become aware when you use gestures and behaviors that may be ineffective.

CREATE 'LETTER-PERFECT' WRITING

Your language, writing style, and tone should be appropriate for the individual who will be reading any document you create.

Here's a test, based on *The Perfect Memo/Write Your Way to Career Success* (Jist Works) by Patricia Westheimer, that you can use while proofreading to make sure each letter or memo you write is just right. Answer **YES** or **NO**:

	YES	NO
1. Have I used action verbs to strengthen my writing (for example: *generate, motivate, propose, revise, schedule,* and *streamline*)?	❑	❑
2. Have I cut out the weakest verbs (such as *am, are, be, been, being, could, have, had, was, will,* and *would*)?	❑	❑
3. Have I corrected every misspelled word by using both my computer's spell-checker and the traditional dictionary?	❑	❑
4. Have I corrected any basic errors of grammar?	❑	❑
5. Have I read my document backwards — from bottom to top — in order to catch all possible errors?	❑	❑
6. Have I made the key points I intended to make?	❑	❑
7. Have I asked the key questions I intended to ask?	❑	❑
8. Have I had my final draft checked over by someone whose writing skills I know are sound?	❑	❑
9. Do I feel satisfied with everything about this document — including the way it looks?	❑	❑
10. Have I done a final check by reading it out loud to see if it sounds just right?	❑	❑

IS YOUR WRITING LETTER-PERFECT? If you answered **YES** to all 10 of the above questions, then your letter is ready for your signature. Since the written word is so permanent, errors will stand out. Only a perfect score is acceptable. If you answered **NO** to any question, review your response. Incorporate the suggestion made in the question into your future correspondence. Take the quiz again in one month, then again in three months. Keep reviewing your scores and improving until you've scored a perfect 10. That's the essential step you need to take in order to make the document you've written letter-perfect.

PUT YOUR WRITING SKILLS TO THE TEST

Writing is as important a business skill today as it ever was. If you think your writing needs no improvement, you may be wrong. Many employees have below-par writing skills. To analyze your own, take the following test, excerpted from materials published by International Writing Institute, Inc., in Cleveland.

In Nos. 1–3, each sentence is grammatically correct. Select the version you consider the best form of communication:

1. (A) The job was done badly.
   (B) The execution was lacking in quality.

2. (A) Kendall is the only person he spoke to.
   (B) Kendall is the only person to whom he spoke.

3. (A) There is limited market potential for used aircraft.
   (B) The market for used aircraft is small.

In Nos. 4–6, choose the answer you consider correct:

4. The best way to organize a report is to:

   (A) Build up to the conclusions, presenting the ideas that support them in a logical order.

   (B) Present the conclusions first, then explain how you reached them.

5. The most effective way to avoid sexism in writing is to:

   (A) Switch to the plural.

   (B) Avoid personal references in either sex.

   (C) Write "he or she."

6. The shorter a sentence is, the harder it hits.

   (A) True   (B) False

YOUR ANSWERS SHOULD HAVE BEEN: 1. (A); 2. (A); 3. (B); 4. (B); 5. (A); 6. (A). Remember, good writing will get you noticed as a strong communicator and a positive representative of your organization. But, like any lifelong skill, it takes practice at every level.

LISTENING SKILLS PAY OFF

It pays to develop good listening skills. Careful listening makes your job easier, promotes productivity, and encourages cooperation. People gravitate to good listeners because good listeners show they care about others.
Take the following quiz to learn how well you listen:

	YES	NO
1. Do you make a special effort to stop what you are doing when someone talks to you?	☐	☐
2. Do you respect a person's remarks, even if you don't care for the individual personally?	☐	☐
3. Do you always give your complete attention when someone is speaking to you?	☐	☐
4. If you are unable to give your full attention at a particular time, do you set another time to meet?	☐	☐
5. Do you try to listen for feelings as well as for facts?	☐	☐
6. To help you understand better, do you ask questions to clarify the speaker's message?	☐	☐
7. Do you let a person finish speaking, even though you can guess what he or she is going to say?	☐	☐
8. Do you try to summarize the person's message as he or she talks instead of interrupting to retort?	☐	☐
9. When someone has confided in you, do you make sure to maintain confidentiality?	☐	☐
10. Do you consciously practice active listening skills to become a better listener?	☐	☐

TOTAL NUMBER OF YES ANSWERS _____

HOW WELL DO YOU LISTEN? If your **YES** answers total eight or more, you are an excellent listener. Five to seven **YES** answers can be considered an average score on this quiz. Any score below this suggests you need to refine your listening skills. Try stopping other activities, paraphrasing what is being said, and acknowledging the speaker's feelings to improve your listening skills.

ASSESS YOUR LISTENING LEVEL

Develop your listening skills by determining your listening level. Once you identify any problems you can decide how to improve the situation. Take the following quiz, responding **YES** or **NO** to each statement to see how your listening level rates:

	YES	NO
1. Your listening skills are selective, picking up only what you need to hear.	☐	☐
2. You find it difficult to listen to certain co-workers whom you don't like on a personal level.	☐	☐
3. You anticipate what peers are going to say.	☐	☐
4. You try to identify others' motives for what they are saying.	☐	☐
5. While peers are speaking, you often make mental notes of things you need to do when you get back to work.	☐	☐
6. You avoid direct eye contact with speakers, so as not to distract them.	☐	☐
7. Your level of attentiveness changes depending upon the speaker's job title and the topic of discussion.	☐	☐
8. You take copious notes about what colleagues say.	☐	☐
9. You determine the basic point of peers' messages as quickly as possible.	☐	☐
10. You formulate your responses while others are speaking.	☐	☐

ARE YOU LISTENING? Every **YES** response is just one way in which you aren't listening as effectively as you could. Good listening requires giving your full, unbiased attention — ears, eyes, and mind — to everyone, regardless of who they are, what they are saying, or how directly their message affects you. Use the results of this quiz as a catalyst for improved listening.

2 STRIKES ON TEAM LISTENING SKILLS

Training consultant James G. Patterson, author of *How to Become a Better Negotiator* (AMACOM), contends that virtually all workplace failures are caused by miscommunication. And miscommunication is very often the result of poor listening habits.

If your teammates don't believe that their listening skills could be at fault, put them to the test. Have each one — including yourself — score the following statements. Then, because people often don't recognize their own shortcomings, have everyone draw a teammate's name out of a hat and anonymously rate that person on these same statements. Use the following scale:

2=ALMOST ALWAYS; 4=USUALLY; 6=SOMETIMES; 8=SELDOM; 10=ALMOST NEVER

1. I label the subject matter of discussions uninteresting. _____
2. I criticize the speaker's delivery or mannerisms. _____
3. I overreact to something the speaker says. _____
4. I listen primarily for the facts. _____
5. I try to outline everything that's said. _____
6. I fake attention to the speaker. _____
7. I allow myself to be distracted easily. _____
8. I let my emotions get the better of me. _____
9. I avoid listening intently to difficult material. _____
10. I daydream instead of paying attention. _____

YOUR TOTAL SCORE _____

HOW WELL DO YOU LISTEN? A score of 80–100 indicates an excellent listener. A score of 20–40 indicates that a good deal of work is needed on listening skills. Patterson says that team leaders usually score around 60, so you can use this as a kind of benchmark.

After each team member scores him- or herself on the above statements, collect and pass out the anonymous critiques. Let people see how others view their listening skills, and they may realize that they aren't quite perfect. Use this exercise as an opportunity to improve the overall communication atmosphere in the team through better listening. Strive to eliminate the **ALMOST ALWAYS** and *USUALLY* responses to prevent your team from getting its third and final strike.

SPEAKING IN FRONT OF A GROUP

Many employees at one time or another, are called upon to make presentations Your goal as a speaker is to send a clear message and have it be heard. Of course, you also want to make a positive impression on your listeners and get them to accept that you are competent, expert, and perhaps even entertaining.

Check to see if you do the following action items before making a presentation:

	YES	NO
1. Do you prepare and use appropriate visual aids to highlight important points you want to make?	☐	☐
2. Do you rehearse your presentation in front of a mirror or on videotape?	☐	☐
3. Do you always check the audiovisual equipment before you begin speaking?	☐	☐
4. Do you gesticulate in a natural manner to emphasize points you want to make?	☐	☐
5. Do you use cue cards to guide your presentation instead of reading from them (which is usually boring)?	☐	☐
6. Do you use humor that involves a personal experience or anecdotes and analogies that apply directly to your message?	☐	☐
7. Do you organize the content of your presentation to be logical and persuasive?	☐	☐
8. Do you look at one listener long enough to deliver a complete thought, then move to another person, and repeat the process?	☐	☐
9. Do you say, "I don't know, but I'll get the information to you later" when you don't know the answer to a question?	☐	☐
10. Do you recap key points and briefly summarize your talk at its end?	☐	☐

HOW DID YOU SCORE ON THE CHECKLIST? Add up the total number of **YES** answers. A score of eight or higher shows you are knowledgeable about public speaking procedures.

READY, TELEPHONES? HERE I COME!

There are a few things you can do each day to "shape up" before making your first phone call. Answer each question below **YES** or **NO**. Your responses will help you evaluate how well you're preparing yourself for your workday.

	YES	NO
1. At the start of your day, do you clear your work space of unneeded papers, magazines, and memos?	☐	☐
2. Do you have a good stock of sharpened pencils, pens, and paper close at hand?	☐	☐
3. Do you check your voice mailbox and return any calls that came in since your last shift?	☐	☐
4. Before you take your first call, do you check the fax machine to see if any overnight faxes arrived?	☐	☐
5. Do you get enough sleep each night, so you're fresh and alert during the day?	☐	☐
6. Do you "dress for success," putting on clean, freshly pressed clothes that help you feel as professional as you are?	☐	☐
7. Do you make sure you have a nutritious breakfast before you leave the house?	☐	☐
8. Do you read the newspaper, a favorite magazine, or a chapter of a book before starting work, so your brain is "up and running" when you're ready to begin?	☐	☐
9. Do you do some throat or voice exercises so you eliminate your groggy morning voice before you pick up the phone?	☐	☐
10. Do you take part in some exercise — stretching, walking, jogging — at the start of the day?	☐	☐

TOTAL NUMBER OF YES ANSWERS _____

SCORE YOURSELF: A score of eight to 10 **YES** answers is a good indication that you're in the best shape physically and mentally before you begin work. Seven is acceptable but, if you scored any lower, you need to adapt some of the suggestions from each question into your daily routine.

BE A PHONE NUMBER DETECTIVE

Some calls to directory service are unavoidable. But being prepared and utilizing some current computer technology make many of these calls unnecessary. Answer the following questions to see what sources you've already explored:

		YES	NO
1.	Do you keep frequently called numbers stored in your telephone memory?	☐	☐
2.	Do you use an address and phone number program in your computer?	☐	☐
3.	When you receive change-of-address information, do you immediately update telephone numbers, too?	☐	☐
4.	Do you know that some phone companies will provide two numbers for the same cost as one when you dial directory assistance?	☐	☐
5.	Are there sufficient copies of the telephone directory available for everyone in your office to use conveniently?	☐	☐
6.	Do you discard outdated telephone books when the new ones arrive?	☐	☐
7.	Do you know you can buy CD-ROM disks that store thousands of phone numbers (business and residential) for easy access?	☐	☐
8.	Do you write down numbers instead of counting on your memory?	☐	☐
9.	Do you notify co-workers of important new telephone numbers?	☐	☐
10.	Can you block calls to directory assistance from your phone (to avoid temptation!)?	☐	☐

TOTAL NUMBER OF YES ANSWERS _____

ARE YOU A GOOD PHONE NUMBER DETECTIVE? A score of eight to 10 **YES** answers illustrates that you already are making great efforts to keep directory assistance charges down. A score of seven or less suggests that you could be doing more.

TAKING CHARGE OF THE TELEPHONE

Because the telephone has been with us so long, we've come to take it for granted. It's easy to overlook just how important effective telephone techniques can be. Here's a test that can hone your telephone skills. Answer each question **YES** or **NO**; then score yourself below:

		YES	NO
1.	When a co-worker's phone is ringing, but she is away from her desk, do you pick up the call quickly?	❏	❏
2.	When the person a caller asks for is not available, do you ask, "Is there any way I can help you?"	❏	❏
3.	Do you answer your own phone promptly?	❏	❏
4.	Do you let management know about problems that callers report to you (such as faulty voice mail)?	❏	❏
5.	If a lot of callers ask the same question about a price or product, do you inform management?	❏	❏
6.	Do you change your voice-mail message daily ("It is December 5, and I will be in the office all day....")?	❏	❏
7.	Immediately after your greeting, do you say to callers, "How may I help you today?"	❏	❏
8.	Do you try to take calls as they come in, rather than allow them to bounce to voice mail?	❏	❏
9.	When you do get a voice-mail message, do you respond promptly?	❏	❏
10.	Do you leave voice-mail messages that provide all the information the other party needs?	❏	❏
11.	If you are going to be away, do you let customers know where they can reach you?	❏	❏
12.	Do you respond to every message before you leave work for the day?	❏	❏

TOTAL NUMBER OF YES ANSWERS _____

DO YOU TAKE CHARGE? If you answered **YES** to 11 or 12 questions, you have taken full control of the telephone, using it as a valuable tool to serve customers and to help your professional standing. Ten is average, but if you answered **YES** to nine or fewer, you need to turn up the amps on your telephone skills.

DOES YOUR GRAMMAR NEED A LITTLE IMPROVEMENT?

Language experts agree that poor speaking habits can be changed with persistence and a plan. This quiz can help you form such a plan. Answer each question **YES** or **NO**; then check your score below:

	YES	NO
1. Do you look for one or two aspects of your speech that need to be changed?	☐	☐
2. Do you use a book of grammar to find correct usage and pronunciation?	☐	☐
3. Do you then use the correct words or forms of speech?	☐	☐
4. When you make a mistake, do you correct yourself?	☐	☐
5. Do you listen closely to how other people speak?	☐	☐
6. When you hear someone use a word unfamiliar to you, do you look it up and then use it yourself?	☐	☐
7. Do you try to increase your vocabulary on a regular basis?	☐	☐
8. Do you do your best to stick with an action plan, even when you become discouraged?	☐	☐
9. Do you keep a written journal of areas in which you need to improve as you uncover them?	☐	☐
10. Do you also keep tabs on the improvements you are making?	☐	☐

TOTAL NUMBER OF YES ANSWERS _____

HOW WELL DO YOU WATCH YOUR WORDS? If all of your answers are **YES**, you deserve a pat on the back! You're already taking serious steps toward strengthening your grammar and vocabulary. Eight to nine **YES** answers are good. Look for ways to change your behavior so that the negatives become positives. But if you scored fewer than eight, you may be making only a haphazard effort to improve. Develop a plan of action and stick with it. Monitor progress. As you improve, you will find that your confidence in everyday speech will grow.

GREAT GREETINGS

First impressions leave lasting impressions on callers, so it's important to be conscious of how we answer the phone. The following quiz can help you get your calls off to a more positive (and productive) start. Answer each question **YES** or **NO**, and then score yourself below:

		YES	NO
1.	Do you answer the phone quickly enough — within two or three rings?	☐	☐
2.	Do you avoid answering too quickly — on the first ring — before callers have had time to really collect their thoughts?	☐	☐
3.	Do you speak loudly and clearly?	☐	☐
4.	Do you offer a complete greeting (one that includes your name, your company's name, and a cheerful "How may I help you?")?	☐	☐
5.	Do you use the customer's name early in the conversation?	☐	☐
6.	Do you treat the call as the most important one of the day?	☐	☐
7.	Do you avoid putting the caller on hold?	☐	☐
8.	If you must use hold, do you keep the caller waiting for as little time as possible?	☐	☐
9.	Do you try to answer the customer's questions yourself before passing the call on to someone else?	☐	☐
10.	Do you thank every customer for calling?	☐	☐

TOTAL NUMBER OF YES ANSWERS _____

HOW POSITIVE ARE YOUR GREETINGS? Nine or 10 **YES** answers indicate that you're sending a positive first impression to callers. Any lower score suggests you need to put a more conscious effort into how you answer the phone. Change your behavior to reflect the suggestions implied by each question. Monitor your improvement by retesting yourself every week until positive first impressions become a habit. Finally, learn ways to motivate yourself so that you're *sure* you are as positive about each call as you possibly can be. For example, try putting a motivational quote near the phone.

WATCH YOUR E-MAIL MANNERS

Do you need to develop a knowledge of the fine points of e-mail etiquette? The following test was prepared by Ann Marie Sabath of At Ease, Inc., in Cincinnati. It originally was published in *Communication Briefings*. Check each response that you think is correct:

1. What should be included in the header of an e-mail message?
   (A) The sender's e-mail address; (B) The receiver's e-mail address; (C) The subject of the message; (D) All of the above.

2. How can you decide which e-mail to read first?
   (A) By the one-line summary in the message header; (B) By the people you like best; (C) By the e-mail addresses that you recognize; (D) By the responsiveness of the people who send you messages.

3. What words should you include in the first sentence of the body of your message?
   (A) "Dear" and the receiver's name; (B) The receiver's name; (C) Your organization's name; (D) The name of the receiver's organization.

4. What's the appropriate message length?
   (A) Between 650 and 950 words; (B) Four to five screens; (C) One or two screens; (D) Any of the above.

5. How frequently should you check your e-mail box?
   (A) At least once an hour; (B) At least twice a day; (C) At least once a day; (D) At least once a month.

YOUR E-MAIL MANNERS: Even without formal etiquette schooling, you're on top of the e-mail game with these answers: 1. (D); 2. (A); 3. (B); 4. (C); and 5. (C). Keep e-mail short; remember, the recipient is probably working his or her way through a whole "stack" of messages. It's OK to use e-mail to write an informal "Nice job" type of message, but remember that the courts have repeatedly ruled that e-mail belongs to your company. Don't use it for nasty e-mails, off-color jokes, or anything else you wouldn't want others to see. Keep in mind that most organizations keep backups of all e-mails (even ones you think you deleted). They defend this practice as a means of protecting the organization in the event of a potential lawsuit down the line. Keep the tone and content as professional as all your other business communication.

COMMUNICATION EDUCATION

Are you able to convey information clearly? The test that follows is based on one that Robert B. Maddux wrote for *Team Building* (Crisp Publications). Answer **TRUE** or **FALSE** after each statement:

		TRUE	FALSE
1.	Messages are most easily understood when you use your full command of the language.	☐	☐
2.	Complex information is best absorbed when you ask the listener to pay close attention.	☐	☐
3.	Key concepts are better remembered when you use repetition to enforce them.	☐	☐
4.	Organizing a message before transmitting it often takes more time than it's worth.	☐	☐
5.	You can determine the receiver's comprehension by asking if he or she understands.	☐	☐
6.	Listening is most effective when you focus on the speaker and what's being said.	☐	☐
7.	Understanding is easier when you suspend judgment until the speaker finishes the message.	☐	☐
8.	Listening comprehension can be improved if you periodically paraphrase the message.	☐	☐
9.	Good listeners ask questions when they don't understand everything.	☐	☐
10.	Message delivery is enhanced by eye contact.	☐	☐

COMMUNICATION ABILITY: Statements 1, 2, 4, and 5 are **FALSE**. The others are **TRUE**. These are the reasons for the **FALSE** answers: (1) Use language that the *receiver* understands; (2) By using specific examples, you'll get attention without asking for it; (4) Organization is essential; and (5) Ask for a paraphrase of what you've said, not a "Yes" or "No" response. If you are conscious of how you communicate, you will begin to see areas where you need to improve.

ASSESS YOUR COMMUNICATION HABITS

Effective group communication should accomplish three things, according to Thomas L. Quick, writing in *Successful Team Building* (AMACOM): (1) share information; (2) provide feedback; and (3) encourage participation among all participants. To determine if your meetings are accomplishing these goals, take the following quiz based on one from Quick's book:

		TRUE	FALSE
1.	Many of our group members avoid direct confrontations but gossip about each other.	☐	☐
2.	Critical feedback destroys morale.	☐	☐
3.	We engage in a lot of "yes, but"-ing.	☐	☐
4.	We use humor to brush off unpleasant truths.	☐	☐
5.	When members are the butt of frequent jokes, they are expected to be good sports about it.	☐	☐
6.	Even when visibly upset, some participants deny having any strong emotions.	☐	☐
7.	When conflict arises, past mistakes are sometimes brought into discussion.	☐	☐
8.	In group discussion, it often seems that participants are addressing different issues.	☐	☐
9.	If a complaint is raised, we always try to find the positive side of the situation.	☐	☐
10.	In problem-solving sessions, members want to affix blame before discussing solutions.	☐	☐

COMMUNICATION RATING: FALSE is the correct response to each question. The key to communication is to address issues honestly and directly. For example, even though it may sound like a good idea to look for the positive side of complaints, as question No. 9 suggests, it's better to address the complaint honestly, deal with it, and move on. Sugar-coating it will only lead to bigger problems.

CHAPTER 2
TEAM SKILLS
TEST YOUR TOGETHERNESS

Motivation, leadership, communication, goal setting, cooperation, and decision making are essential skills for a successful team. How well a team functions in these areas will determine its success. Rather than leaving a team's success to chance after all the time, money, and effort that has been put into the team-building process, it makes sense to conduct ongoing evaluations of team progress and performance.

Take a moment to reflect on your team's performance and attitudes.

Could some of your team members use a little help with their motivation? Use the quiz "Morale a Must in the Workplace" to get tips on how to boost team spirit and help restore a positive team environment.

Are unfocused discussions taking up too much meeting time? Do members seem to have a difficult time solving problems? "The Art of Team Discussions" is a quiz that can help team members evaluate how well they contribute to effective team discussions and provides them with ideas on how to handle conflicts that can cause to team problems.

Are all of your team members contributing to the team's professional and personal development? Have team members use the quiz "Overcome Obstacles, Get Involved" to assess their roles as team developers by rating themselves on how well they support teammates and praise their accomplishments.

These and other quizzes in this chapter provide team leaders, managers, and trainers with the tools to track and evaluate the 'forming, storming, norming, and performing' stages of team development. Quiz results allow you to measure team progress, identify strengths, reveal areas of weakness, and test learning and skills retention.

As the role of teams expand, the importance of team-building increases. Team building requires a knowledge of group dynamics, the ability to translate company objectives into realistic team goals, and the talent to inspire a diverse group of individuals to work together to achieve those goals. It takes time and money to train and develop an effective team, establish team goals and ground rules, and promote team spirit. Quizzes are an excellent way to measure the success of your team and to encourage team performance improvement.

HAS TEAM SPIRIT INVADED YOUR SOUL?

Applying team spirit to a traditionally structured or hierarchical organization will certainly change the corporate culture — for the better. Employees become empowered when companies promote team spirit, says David Cleland, author of *Teams and the Competitive Edge* (John Wiley & Sons, Inc.). When that happens, employees feel more satisfaction in their work and take on more responsibility. This shift will spur the change in corporate culture that you're looking for.

To determine if team spirit has affected your corporate culture, respond **YES, SOMETIMES,** or **NO** to the following statements:

1. We expect to participate in developing and implementing strategies for our company. _____

2. We feel that our opinions are valued and that we have access to key information on the company's performance. _____

3. We are treated as thinking adults in our organization. _____

4. Our company encourages creativity — it's OK to make mistakes. _____

5. Everyone in our company has close contact with suppliers and customers. _____

6. Our company fosters a culture of equality — no special perks, such as reserved parking and executive dining. _____

7. There is a high degree of interdependence among everyone, with a recognition that everyone contributes to the company's success. _____

8. Everyone is responsible for quality at all times. _____

9. Most employees are cross-trained in more than one job. _____

HAS THE SPIRIT MOVED YOU? If team spirit has really taken hold in your corporate culture, your answers should be mostly **YES** and **SOMETIMES.** Remember, however, to allow time for the transition to take place. You and your colleagues need to be open to change and willing to try new procedures in order to take advantage of the opportunity provided to you.

TRANSITION TO INTERDEPENDENCE

One of the most important traits required to work in an interdependent environment is trust and mutual respect. But this doesn't always come naturally to everyone — especially people who have been taught to protect their turf in hyper-competitive organizations. To gain the team spirit, start by determining how far you have to go to achieve it. Respond **YES** or **NO** to the following statements and score yourself below:

		YES	NO
1.	I share newly acquired data or information with my peers.	☐	☐
2.	I realize that what's best for me may not always be what's best for my team or my organization.	☐	☐
3.	I listen to others' ideas more than I talk about my own.	☐	☐
4.	I am willing to train my colleagues in areas where I have expertise.	☐	☐
5.	I can find individual enjoyment or satisfaction in recognition bestowed upon my department or team.	☐	☐
6.	I know how my job function affects the jobs of my peers.	☐	☐
7.	I accept my responsibility in meeting group deadlines.	☐	☐
8.	I am eager to compliment my colleagues on their work when it is deserved.	☐	☐
9.	I can give and receive constructive feedback — even when it isn't complimentary.	☐	☐
10.	I support my co-workers in their pursuit of success and seek their help in my own struggles.	☐	☐

TOTAL NUMBER OF YES ANSWERS _____

WHAT'S YOUR SCORE? An experienced team-oriented employee should answer **YES** to at least eight of these statements, with a perfect 10 being the goal. But don't be worried if your score was lower. You need to relearn how you relate with your colleagues to achieve a team spirit. Study each of these statements and strive to succeed in these areas of interdependence. Explain to your peers why you may be having a difficult transition, and look to them for support.

DOES YOUR TEAM STICK TOGETHER?

Teams that stick together outperform other work groups. This essential quality is cohesiveness, which refers to the likability, acceptance, and respect felt by team members for each other. Like good morale, its elusive nature can't be ordered by team leaders. Only the team itself can improve or detract from its "stick together" power. Take this quiz to see if your team is adding cohesiveness to its achievements:

		YES	NO
1.	Members of my team are good at confronting and negotiating differences.	☐	☐
2.	My peers are technically skilled to perform well.	☐	☐
3.	We are quick to share ideas and feelings with each other.	☐	☐
4.	All opinions are respected, even unpopular ones.	☐	☐
5.	Being on our team increases my self-confidence.	☐	☐
6.	I can honestly evaluate my team performance.	☐	☐
7.	My team values openness, honesty, and trust.	☐	☐
8.	We encourage a healthy dose of peer feedback.	☐	☐
9.	We work on building self-esteem and integrity as well as productivity.	☐	☐
10.	We are all committed to doing anything necessary to achieve our goals.	☐	☐

TOTAL NUMBER OF YES ANSWERS _____

YOUR COHESIVENESS QUOTIENT: A score of seven or more **YES** answers represents superior performance. Your team works together as one productive, thinking machine. Five or six is average. Anything lower suggests problems with your team spirit. Focus on improving one of these behaviors at a time until you're stuck like glue.

OVERCOME OBSTACLES, GET INVOLVED

If not everyone on your team contributes to group projects, there may be obstacles standing in the way of employee involvement.

To avoid this situation, make sure there aren't any obstacles keeping you and your teammates from giving challenges your best attempt. Answer the following questions, based on suggestions from Merck Cherokee in Danville, Pennsylvania. Your responses should identify what's blocking some team members from getting involved:

		YES	NO
1.	Do you encourage new members to get involved in team activities from the start?	☐	☐
2.	Do you allow time to deal with conflicts or disagreements within the team?	☐	☐
3.	When motivation is low, do you try to energize and encourage your teammates?	☐	☐
4.	Are you always honest and sincere with your peers and team leaders?	☐	☐
5.	Do you and your teammates have respect and consideration for one another's perspectives and concerns?	☐	☐
6.	Does your team have a common purpose that everyone can rally behind?	☐	☐
7.	Does your team hold regular "retreats" — both on- and off-site — to discuss in-depth concerns and goals?	☐	☐
8.	Do you share all information with teammates?	☐	☐
9.	Are all team members attending and contributing to meetings within the organization?	☐	☐
10.	Do you seek help from teammates and leaders when you are caught in a bind?	☐	☐

TOTAL NUMBER OF YES ANSWERS _____

WHAT'S YOUR SCORE? Eight or more **YES** responses are an indication of proactive involvement in team activities. You don't allow obstacles to stand in your way of contributing to every team project. If you scored lower, you need to work on adjusting your attitude and becoming more of a team player.

CURE CROSS-FUNCTIONAL ANXIETY

Working on a cross-functional team allows you to see work issues from many perspectives. Also, your own skills will be tested as your team's "expert" in your field. Assess your potential for cross-functional success by taking this test, based on one by Andrew J. DuBrin, Ph.D. DuBrin, Ph.D., author of *The Breakthrough Team Player* (AMACOM). Give yourself a score for each statement according to this code:

1 = STRONGLY AGREE; 2 = AGREE; 3 = NEUTRAL; 4 = DISAGREE; 5 = STRONGLY DISAGREE

1. It's best to stick to your specialty and not try to spread yourself thin in other areas. _____

2. I don't care to learn about what other teams are doing. _____

3. I seldom talk to people whose work is different from mine. _____

4. When assigned new team projects, I think first about how they will affect my career. _____

5. My philosophy is: "It's not what you can do for your company, but what your company can do for you." _____

6. People from different fields can't discuss technical problems. _____

7. The best judgments come from team people who concentrate their energies in one skill area. _____

8. Team members lose their edge when they can't focus on one specialty. _____

9. Superior solutions come only when people from the same field get together. _____

10. I find working with those who share my interests and expertise more fulfilling than with peers from other areas. _____

YOUR TOTAL SCORE _____

YOUR CROSS-POTENTIAL: DuBrin's assessment: With a score of **45–50**, your mind-set is perfect for working on a multitalented team. At **25–44**, you have some reservations, but you should be able to work through them. A lower score indicates that you're bound to your "function." Try a broader team outlook.

MORALE A MUST IN THE WORKPLACE

Each team member is affected by the attitudes, behaviors, and performances of other co-workers. There may be times, for example, when the morale of a teammate may not be up to par. Therefore, it may be your responsibility to try to bolster that sagging spirit. The following quiz will give you some idea of how effective you are at boosting team morale:

	YES	NO
1. Are you interested in doing whatever you can to keep team morale up at all times?	☐	☐
2. Do you reflexively counter other people's negative statements (without getting into an argument)?	☐	☐
3. Do you try to encourage other people through your own exemplary behavior?	☐	☐
4. Are you quick to assure disenchanted team members of your willingness to help them whenever needed?	☐	☐
5. Do you intervene quickly when you see morale sagging, before it becomes a downward spiral?	☐	☐
6. Do you raise morale-related issues during meetings?	☐	☐
7. When co-workers suggest that a job is too hard, do you point out examples of similar jobs that had successful outcomes?	☐	☐
8. Do you compliment your team members on work well done?	☐	☐
9. When co-workers fail at a project, do you encourage them to make another attempt and stay motivated?	☐	☐
10. Do you point out that if management didn't think your team could handle a challenging job, they wouldn't have assigned it in the first place?	☐	☐

YOUR SCORE: If you answered YES to each of the above questions, then you are the person the group depends on to keep the mood positive and productive. But if your score is lower, reconsider your attitude in the workplace. Try increasing positive statements made toward co-workers. Set goals for yourself, and work on one weak point every day. Observing the new and improved team morale will encourage you to continue with this behavior.

GETTING COMMITMENT FROM ALL TEAM MEMBERS

Lack of cooperation may be the result of a "de-motivating" team dynamic. The following quiz may help you find out if a problem exists. Answer **YES** or **NO** to each question:

		YES	NO
1.	Do you assign tasks or responsibilities that truly interest each team member?	☐	☐
2.	Are team members fully aware of one another's strengths?	☐	☐
3.	As a group, do you draw on those strengths in making assignments?	☐	☐
4.	Are individuals able to use their key skills and expertise for team activities?	☐	☐
5.	Does everyone listen when others — even the shy or introverted — express their ideas and opinions?	☐	☐
6.	Do the reluctant team members seem to get as much praise and recognition when they do make a contribution as other team members?	☐	☐
7.	Does everyone get full credit where it counts most — in reports to management, for instance?	☐	☐
8.	Are all team members regularly included in the more high-profile or prestige tasks that draw recognition for the group?	☐	☐
9.	Do you all have equal access to resources, such as information, equipment, and assistance?	☐	☐
10.	Does everyone on the team receive regular feedback on performance?	☐	☐

TOTAL NUMBER OF YES ANSWERS   _____

HOW DO YOU RATE AS A MOTIVATOR? If you scored fewer than nine **YES** answers, current team dynamics may not be offering enough motivation for everyone in the group. Review all of the above questions for clues as to how the reluctant joiners in particular could be encouraged to participate more actively and wholeheartedly.

CLIMBING TEAMWORK SKILLS LADDER

At Eastman Kodak Company, teamwork has such a high priority that management has developed a "ladder" of team skills to distinguish those employees proficient in team abilities from entry-level novices. Andrew J. DuBrin, Ph.D., author of *The Breakthrough Team Player* (AMACOM), uses the Kodak ladder as a model to help team members evaluate their own levels of competency. To measure your own level, read the following statements. Then check either **N** to indicate that you have that competence *now* or **I** to show that you must *improve* your performance:

N I

1. I attend team meetings regularly. ☐ ☐
2. I participate in brainstorming. ☐ ☐
3. I share information with everyone. ☐ ☐
4. I'm a good facilitator. ☐ ☐
5. I always cooperate to bring about team success. ☐ ☐
6. I trust my teammates. ☐ ☐
7. I work to develop a consensus among team members. ☐ ☐
8. I'm a good teacher and learner. ☐ ☐
9. I have strong leadership skills. ☐ ☐
10. I place conflict resolution high on any list of team basics. ☐ ☐
11. I make original contributions to team success and build on others' contributions. ☐ ☐
12. I'm always eager to help form special teams. ☐ ☐
13. I work actively to establish the team's direction and goals. ☐ ☐
14. Through positive actions, I often challenge the views of others. ☐ ☐
15. I work to promote team unity. ☐ ☐
16. When necessary, I'll help lighten a teammate's workload. ☐ ☐

YOUR RUNG ON THE LADDER: Make sure you try to improve on your weak areas, but always maintain the effective interpersonal work skills that benefit you and your team members. Over time, and by learning from your fellow teammates, you will steadily move up the teamwork ladder.

GROWTH CATALYST OR OBSTACLE?

As an active part of the team, your leader will want you to be a catalyst for growth, spurring the team's progress along with your ideas and contributions. If you don't take this stance, then you'll become "deadweight," slowing the team down and acting as an obstacle to its success. To see if you are a catalyst or an obstacle to team success, study the following characteristics of each, based on a list created by Development Dimensions International, Inc. Place a check in the box next to the behaviors that best describe you:

CATALYST

- ☐ Ask, listen, and learn
- ☐ Recognize and solve problems

- ☐ Provide balanced feedback
- ☐ Share thoughts and knowledge
- ☐ Promote team by sharing successes
- ☐ Focus on potential
- ☐ Innovate, create
- ☐ Support others' efforts
- ☐ Ask for input
- ☐ Build trust and commitment

- ☐ Have team-centered outlook

OBSTACLE

- ☐ Tell and assume
- ☐ Identify problems, mandate solutions

- ☐ Criticize
- ☐ Withhold data
- ☐ Wait for others to notice successes
- ☐ Focus on limits
- ☐ Maintain status quo
- ☐ Do it all alone
- ☐ Have all the answers
- ☐ Use threats and intimidation

- ☐ Have self-centered outlook

CATALYST OR OBSTACLE? You need only look at the location of the check marks to see where your team behaviors are concentrated. Your leader is right — if you aren't actively pushing the team to new heights through your own actions and your support of others' work, then you are holding the group back.

Take this exercise further by writing down what you see as the "benefits" of all the actions you have placed a check next to — even those in the "Obstacles" column. You're likely to notice that any benefits to being an obstacle are short-term and ultimately could be destructive to your career. If you're guilty of maintaining the status quo, for example, you won't rock the boat, but you also won't get promoted.

AM I IN A WORK GROUP OR ON A TEAM?

A team has different characteristics from a work group, according to *The Wisdom of Teams* (Harvard Business School Press). Take the following quiz to see where your group fits in. You can also use it as a guide to get your team on track:

1. The leadership role in our team is:
   A. Handled by one strong, clearly focused leader.
   B. Shared by all members.
2. When we are assigned a task:
   A. There is individual accountability.
   B. There is mutual support as well as individual responsibility.
3. Our team purpose is:
   A. The same as the broader organizational mission.
   B. A specific one that the team itself delivers.
4. Members meet high expectations by:
   A. Executing a narrow set of tasks efficiently.
   B. Working together interchangeably on continuous improvement.
5. We all perform our daily jobs by:
   A. Following directives.
   B. Thinking, working, and doing.
6. Our supervisor is important because we:
   A. Rely on managerial control.
   B. Need someone to help us shape our direction.
7. Our attitude is:
   A. A fair day's pay for a fair day's work.
   B. Expand capabilities for personal growth.

SCORE YOURSELF: Give yourself one point for every **A** answer and two points for every **B** answer. If you scored 14, you're functioning as a team. If you scored 10–13, you have some team characteristics and are on the learning curve to become one. If you scored nine or lower, chances are you are in a work group.

NOVICES ASSESS TEAM READINESS

Organizing a formal team to improve efficiency and communication may be the best way to improve your department's performance and productivity. Unfortunately, an inexperienced team often makes hasty decisions and works within a disorganized structure. Valuable time may be lost going back to the drawing board — attempting to put things in order. Avoid this setback by assessing your team readiness.

The following quiz has been adapted from a forum given by teams expert Jean Wilson at the Development Dimensions International 1997 Conference Series in Chicago. It will help you evaluate your team and determine if you and your co-workers are prepared for working together successfully. Respond to each statement with a **YES** or **NO**. Then score yourself below:

	YES	NO
1. I'm able to handle more responsibility and decision-making authority than I currently have.	☐	☐
2. I look for ways in which our team could work more effectively.	☐	☐
3. My co-workers and I teach one another about our jobs, in case we need to fill in for someone.	☐	☐
4. I enjoy learning new tasks or jobs.	☐	☐
5. I can accept ambiguity about my job responsibilities.	☐	☐
6. I realize that it takes time to work out a productive team system.	☐	☐
7. I listen carefully and verify that I understand what my colleagues say.	☐	☐
8. I stay on track and respect everyone's differences.	☐	☐
9. I examine the problem *before* coming up with a solution.	☐	☐
10. I can competently perform my tasks, as well as those of most other team members.	☐	☐

WHAT'S YOUR SCORE? If you responded **YES** to each of the above statements, your team is well on its way to establishing a productive group unit. Meet with your teammates and discuss their results. Work together on alleviating disagreements with the above statements and, if necessary, consult the more experienced teams in your company.

ASSESS TEAM'S PERFORMANCE LEVEL

Teams that are high performers don't wait for others to identify their strengths and weaknesses. They analyze and reanalyze their structure regularly. The following are some key team characteristics taken from a Team Assessment created by PDS, Inc. Check **YES** for each statement that correctly describes your team's behavior and **NO** for those that don't:

	YES	NO
1. Team members are aware of their own work styles and how they affect others.	☐	☐
2. People are "straight" with others on the team, speaking from the heart.	☐	☐
3. Team members keep their commitments to others.	☐	☐
4. You have established guidelines for handling conflicts and use them to deal with "tough issues."	☐	☐
5. Team members are flexible in their individual roles.	☐	☐
6. You have input into the key decisions that affect how your team works.	☐	☐
7. Every team member can clearly communicate your mission statement to customers and managers.	☐	☐
8. When solving a problem, you search for the root causes rather than quick solutions.	☐	☐
9. You have an empowerment plan, detailing what duties will be transferred to whom, by when, and with what training.	☐	☐
10. Your team looks for a better way to do work rather than doing it the same way.	☐	☐
11. You have determined where your team's external relationships with customers, suppliers, and other teams are strong and where they need help.	☐	☐
12. You communicate guidelines and expectations to new team members.	☐	☐

YOUR ASSESSMENT: A high-performance team should respond **YES** to each statement. Use this assessment as a working document. Set goals to achieve related to those areas to which your team responded **NO**. Then establish a plan for how you will reach those goals. An assessment is just the beginning. It's up to your team to make each response a **YES**.

HOW GOOD IS YOUR TEAMWORK?

Teams — like all living things — are in a constant state of change. To make sure that the changes your team is experiencing are good and that it is on the road to its performing phase, you and your team members should regularly evaluate your teamwork.

Answer the following questions, based on an assessment from *Leading Teams: Mastering the New Role*, by John H. Zenger and Associates (Business One Irwin), to identify how well your team functions. Use this scale in your appraisal: **1 = STRONGLY DISAGREE; 2 = DISAGREE; 3 = NO OPINION; 4 = AGREE; 5 = STRONGLY AGREE.**

1. The team knows what it has to get done. _____
2. Team members get charged up from new ideas. _____
3. Everyone expresses his or her viewpoints freely. _____
4. Everybody knows and understands the goals
   and roles of the other members. _____
5. Everyone participates in team decision making. _____
6. We express our feelings. _____
7. There is a great deal of individual respect
   for one another on the team. _____
8. Team members pull together. _____
9. When someone has an opinion, everyone
   listens to it. Nobody prejudges. _____
10. There is very little infighting within the team.
    Conflicts are not avoided, but are resolved. _____

                                              TOTAL _____

HOW WELL DOES YOUR TEAM FUNCTION? Add up the ratings for each of the statements, and then divide the total by 10. According to Zenger, if your score is four or higher, the teamwork within your group is strong. An average of two or lower indicates that something is awry.

How developed is your team?

Maturity in a team setting comes from a number of factors, including time and experience. If your team has been operating for 12 to 18 months and handles most of its new tasks successfully, then it's probably reached a mature stage, according to Jill A. George, Ph.D., and Jeanne M. Wilson, co-authors of *Team Member's Survival Guide* (DDI Press). However, this time line can fluctuate depending, in part, upon the skill levels and commitment of the individual members.

Review the following list of team characteristics and activities, based on materials prepared by George and Wilson. Place a check mark next to each one that applies to your team. Then read the analysis below to determine your team's phase:

1. Developing team goals in alignment with the organizational vision and values. ☐

2. Assuming advanced responsibilities, such as budgeting and peer reviews. ☐

3. Spending time with your former supervisor to gain expertise. ☐

4. Maintaining quality levels at an all-time high. ☐

5. Aligning individual attitudes and behaviors with the team concept. ☐

6. Spending the majority of your time on strategic customer, product, or service improvements. ☐

7. Making more empowered decisions as a team. ☐

8. Noticing that doubts about the team concept have practically disappeared. ☐

9. Gathering information about customer complaints, profitability, and other business matters. ☐

10. Stretching to take on roles outside your department. ☐

TEAM PHASE: Each odd-numbered statement is representative of a newly formed, immature team, while the even-numbered ones apply to mature teams, say the authors. If your team displays a combination of these behaviors, that means you are in a growth phase on your way to reaching maturity. With the experience that only comes from spending time together working as a team, you'll soon reach the stage of high performance.

PREVENT ONSET OF TEAM FATIGUE

"As with many good intentions, it's often easier to start something than it is to sustain any kind of concerted effort," asserts teamwork expert Jeanne Wilson. This philosophy accurately describes the natural progression of most new teams: an impressive beginning and, yet, a lagging trot to the finish line. You can avoid it in your new team if you spot the early indications of team fatigue.

The following quiz, adapted from a forum given by Wilson, will assess your team's stamina. Respond to each question with a **YES** or **NO**. Then score your team below:

	YES	NO
1. We tend to stick with new plans or ideas.	☐	☐
2. Of the ideas we agreed to last year, more than 75 percent are still actively supported by the team.	☐	☐
3. We're better at generating ideas than implementing them.	☐	☐
4. We're good at making lists, but we rarely refer to them.	☐	☐
5. We tend to take on more than we can reasonably handle as a team.	☐	☐
6. If the team misses a deadline, it's usually no big deal.	☐	☐
7. The average time span for our team to remain excited about something is less than three months.	☐	☐
8. If a project lasts longer than three months, our team tends to lose interest.	☐	☐
9. We are very disciplined in using lists to follow up on action items and agreements.	☐	☐
10. We get more satisfaction from generating ideas than from implementing them.	☐	☐

WHAT'S YOUR SCORE? If your team is still going strong, with no indication of letting up, you should have answered **YES** to Statement Nos. 1, 2, and 9 and **NO** to the remainder. Staying focused as a team takes effort. It also requires communication and trust among members. If you answered any questions incorrectly, determine why. This is the starting point to turning around a downward trend.

DON'T HOLD BACK WITH TEAM LEADER

Your relationship with your team leader will shape your entire team experience. Team members can facilitate a productive relationship with their leaders. Here, we'll see how well you do in one important area of leader relations — communication. Respond **TRUE** or **FALSE** to each statement; then score yourself below:

		TRUE	FALSE
1.	I refrain from exaggeration, innuendo, and other bad habits of communication.	☐	☐
2.	I give my team leader solutions to problems, instead of relying on him or her to solve them.	☐	☐
3.	If need be, I can be adept at using humor to defuse potential arguments.	☐	☐
4.	I have taken the time to get to know my leader's moods and how to read them.	☐	☐
5.	I know which forms of communication my leader prefers — memos, e-mail, face-to-face chats.	☐	☐
6.	I never criticize my leader behind his or her back.	☐	☐
7.	I wouldn't undermine my leader's ideas in order to spotlight my own.	☐	☐
8.	I know the best time of day to visit my leader.	☐	☐
9.	I can support my leader's decisions even if I disagree with them if it's for the good of the team.	☐	☐
10.	I alert my leader if I've made a mistake — even if he or she probably won't find out otherwise.	☐	☐

TOTAL NUMBER OF YES ANSWERS   _____

YOUR SCORE: If you responded **TRUE** to nine or 10 statements, then you really know how to communicate with your team leader for your benefit as well as your team's. A score of eight is good, but seven or fewer indicates you could stand to open up those communication lines. If you feel uncomfortable talking to your leader, try to figure out why. Are you afraid that your words might come back to haunt you? Or are you holding back information as a way to gain power? Realize that you're not only hurting yourself by not communicating, you're also making the entire team suffer. Open up.

THE ART OF TEAM DISCUSSIONS

Team members must take responsibility for developing their own discussion skills. And, yes, they are skills. To determine how well you're currently contributing to effective team discussion, and to get some ideas on how to improve this key communication medium, take the following quiz, based on information in *The Team Memory Jogger* (Joiner). Respond with a TRUE or a FALSE to each statement:

	TRUE	FALSE
1. I give reasons for my opinions.	❒	❒
2. I ask others to explain reasons behind their opinions.	❒	❒
3. I help engage other people in discussion by asking for their opinions and ideas.	❒	❒
4. I try to bring the team back on track when discussions digress.	❒	❒
5. I pull together and summarize ideas expressed by my teammates.	❒	❒
6. I suggest methods the team can use to work on issues.	❒	❒
7. I help the team check for agreement by posing questions such as "So, am I correct in saying that we all agree that ...?"	❒	❒
8. I try to find areas of agreement in conflicting points of view.	❒	❒
9. I listen attentively until a teammate has completed a thought before offering my own.	❒	❒
10. I judge the idea being presented and not the person presenting it.	❒	❒

TOTAL NUMBER OF TRUE ANSWERS _____

WHAT'S YOUR SCORE? Eight or more TRUE answers indicate that you play an active role in promoting effective team discussions. But your efforts alone won't be enough to ensure that your team meetings will become more productive and interactive. Each member of the team must employ the techniques listed above to become an expert in the art of discussion.

SHAPING TEAM WITH NEW PEERS

Training new teammates is a great opportunity to shape the direction of your team for the future while improving your own basic skills. Every time you teach a skill to someone else, you invariably become better at it yourself. The following is a checklist of training maxims to adopt as you train new teammates. Read the list and place a check mark next to each statement that is part of your training system:

1. When I give instructions that have multiple steps, I know and explain the objective of each step. ❐

2. I am familiar with all the features of the equipment required to do various jobs. ❐

3. I know our company's mission and understand how our team's goals fit into that picture. ❐

4. I plan my instructions to ensure that steps are presented in the correct, logical order. ❐

5. I find out about a new teammate's work background before starting his or her instruction. ❐

6. I ask the trainee questions in order to tailor the training experience to his or her particular needs. ❐

7. I try to relate a teammate's training to what he or she already knows. ❐

8. I incorporate hands-on training into the program to promote learning by doing. ❐

9. I allow a trainee to get his or her "feet wet," even if it means that mistakes are made. ❐

10. I am quick to praise and encourage the efforts of a novice team player. ❐

WHAT'S YOUR SCORE? Each statement in this checklist represents a training strategy that you should be incorporating into your program for new team members. Current team members should have a hand in developing this important training program, as well. Each one should submit to you a list of items or issues that they feel should be covered in the training process. Meet as a team to determine the most important issues to incorporate, and address how these points should be conveyed. By keeping the entire team involved in this orientation training, you'll have a better chance of developing strong new members.

LIAISON BRINGS TEAMS TOGETHER

Have you been asked to be a team liaison to promote cooperation among various teams in your company? Do you know where to start? Start with yourself — learn to cooperate better in your new role and then lead the way for others. Answer the questions below **YES** or **NO** to see if you're taking steps to position yourself as a true liaison who bridges the gaps between teams and helps everyone to work toward the same goals:

	YES	NO
1. Have you introduced yourself in person to your contacts on other teams?	❑	❑
2. Have you talked to them about their duties so that you understand the daily demands on their time and energy?	❑	❑
3. Have you checked to make sure exactly whom you should contact for certain types of information?	❑	❑
4. Do you understand specifically what people on other teams can — and can't — do for you?	❑	❑
5. Do you know how your team's work affects that of other teams?	❑	❑
6. Do you ever ask what you could do to make colleagues' jobs easier?	❑	❑
7. Do you try to avoid asking for information or assistance during peak times when team members are busiest?	❑	❑
8. Are you gracious and giving, even when others come to you for help at a bad time?	❑	❑
9. Do you see to it that you and your teammates have contact with other teams through meetings?	❑	❑
10. Do you see inter-team cooperation as essential to the health and success of your organization?	❑	❑

TOTAL NUMBER OF YES ANSWERS _____

WHAT'S YOUR SCORE? If you answered **YES** to eight or more questions, you're establishing yourself as a team liaison by forging comfortable, productive relationships among teams. Until you can answer affirmatively to each question, there will be gaps in your team network and, thus, breakdowns in productivity. Work to get a perfect 10.

CHAPTER 3
INTERPERSONAL SKILLS
YOU MAY MARCH TO A DIFFERENT DRUMMER, BUT YOU STILL HAVE TO MARCH

Good interpersonal skills are the cornerstone of success for employees in virtually every job function and business area today. As the team environments gain in importance and ubiquity, so does the need for employees who can work well with others, keep a cool head, manage conflict, handle criticism, and maintain an interest in and commitment to the job.

Tracking employee progress and skills in interpersonal areas is an even taller order. Dartnell makes this tracking easier by providing quizzes that supervisors, managers, and trainers can use to evaluate the people skills that are so essential in the workplace.

How are your people getting along?

A quiz such as "Go for the Win-Win Outcome" is designed to help guide negotiation efforts in a team-based environment. Analyzing their own responses helps employees key in on what may be keeping them from negotiating their way out of a dispute and provides helpful suggestions on how to debate rather than argue and how to compromise and still remain effective.

Have you noticed that some of your employees are having difficulties relating to their supervisors? "Creating Boss Bonds" is a quiz that might help those employees find some insights into forming productive relationships with their bosses. Reviewing their answers can give employees clues on how to nurture and support that bond.

Are you concerned that conflict may be hindering some work relationships? Use the quiz "Keeping Cool When Things Get Hot" to help your employees discover some of the sources that can lead to volatile situations and what behaviors can be used to turn these conflicts into productive working environments.

These and the other quizzes in this chapter can help you and your employees pinpoint workplace issues that arise from interpersonal problems. Taking the time to examine their responses to these quizzes, employees can discover insights on how to give feedback properly in the workplace and deal with negative feelings that affect productivity and team or co-worker morale.

Improving an employee's interpersonal skills is a challenging goal. In most cases it's up to the managers, supervisors, and company trainers to take the time and spend the money to provide the coaching and training that will enable employees to develop or improve their working relationships or change attitudes that keep them from performing at their best. These quizzes can help you analyze your employees' strengths and pinpoint areas where they can increase their effectiveness.

HOW DO YOUR 'PEOPLE SKILLS' RATE?

In addition to your job skills, it takes extraordinary people skills to succeed professionally. That's why it's smart to take an inventory of them. Knowing where your shortcomings lie should enlighten you and lead to any needed improvement. Take the following quiz to see how you score:

		YES	NO
1.	Do you smile and look people in the eye when you meet and talk with them?	☐	☐
2.	Are you genuinely interested in people and what they do personally and professionally?	☐	☐
3.	Do you freely express that personal interest when conversing with others?	☐	☐
4.	Are you considerate of other people's reactions, opinions, and feelings?	☐	☐
5.	Do you have the brand of humor that allows you to see something amusing in almost any situation?	☐	☐
6.	Are you patient with people when they don't have the same skills as you?	☐	☐
7.	Are you a friendly, helpful person? Does helping people make you feel good?	☐	☐
8.	Do you look for the good rather than the bad in other people?	☐	☐
9.	Do you have a generally optimistic outlook on life? Do you share that optimism with others?	☐	☐
10.	Are you generally positive when expressing your views and ideas?	☐	☐

TOTAL NUMBER OF YES ANSWERS _____

HOW DID YOU DO ON THE QUIZ? A score of eight or more **YES** answers is excellent, marking you as likable, perceptive, and sensitive with people. A lower score indicates that you need to become more oriented to other people to make the most of your personal and professional relationships.

BRINGING MORE 'CIVILITY' TO WORK

Civility is the essence of author Jim Lundy's "10 commandments for maintaining good interpersonal relationships." They're outlined in his book *Lead, Follow or Get Out of the Way* (Berkley). Take this quiz, based on his commandments. Respond **YES** or **NO** to each:

		YES	NO
1.	I'm generally friendly and cheerful at work and don't burden others with my personal problems or negativity.	☐	☐
2.	I always make an effort to listen more than I talk.	☐	☐
3.	I pay close attention to the way I speak to co-workers, realizing that how I say something can be even more significant than what I say.	☐	☐
4.	I'm open to others' ideas and opinions — and I know how to disagree without being disagreeable.	☐	☐
5.	I give feedback in a constructive way and praise as much as — or more than — I criticize.	☐	☐
6.	I give others lots of credit when they deserve it, and I don't brag about my own accomplishments.	☐	☐
7.	I avoid making promises I can't keep.	☐	☐
8.	I don't gossip, make negative comments about others, or spread rumors.	☐	☐
9.	I make it a priority to be patient and understanding, and I never hold colleagues or customers up to ridicule.	☐	☐
10.	I have a high regard for my co-workers, respecting their feelings and appreciating their need for self-esteem.	☐	☐

TOTAL NUMBER OF YES ANSWERS _____

WHERE ARE YOU ON THE "CIVILITY SCALE"? Nine or more **YES** responses would indicate that civility is a key element of your working relationships. But perhaps you'd like your co-workers to be more attuned to the need for civility on the job. Why not suggest that the entire group spend a few minutes taking this quiz at an upcoming staff meeting? Then discuss the results — and how you all could be more considerate of one another.

DO YOU GIVE FEEDBACK PROPERLY?

Educators Harriet V. Lawrence and Albert K. Wiswell say that effective feedback is two-way, engaging, responsive, specific, given with empathy and a spirit of inquiry, and directed toward a desired outcome. The following test is based on one that they wrote for *Training & Development*. Respond to each statement with **RARELY**, **SOMETIMES**, or **OFTEN**:

1. I limit my feedback to specific skills that others can do something about. _____

2. I avoid one-way feedback by asking others about their concerns. _____

3. I provide positive as well as negative feedback to motivate others. _____

4. When giving feedback, I focus on tasks and behaviors rather than personalities. _____

5. I avoid "saving up" criticisms so that I can unload them all at once. _____

6. I try to understand feedback from my colleagues' points of view. _____

7. I avoid giving feedback when I'm angry, busy, or tired. _____

8. I refrain from using sarcasm. _____

9. I encourage others to ask questions, and I don't interrupt them. _____

10. I listen patiently to others' needs. _____

11. I pick the right time and place to give feedback. _____

12. I stress the need to share goals when giving feedback. _____

TOTAL SCORE _____

FEEDBACK SKILLS AND FLAWS: Give yourself five points for each statement that you marked **OFTEN**, three for each **SOMETIMES**, and one for each **RARELY**. A score of 55 or more indicates that you have very strong feedback skills. If you scored lower, focus on the behaviors that you rarely exhibit to start. Once you practice them on a more regular basis, move on to the **SOMETIMES** responses. Good feedback takes practice, so get started today.

IS THERE A GOOD WAY TO GIVE UNSOLICITED ADVICE?

None of us likes to be told we're doing something wrong — unless we ask for the advice. And, yet, if you already have a good working relationship with someone, should you stand back and let them "harm" themselves when you could help by speaking up? Probably not.

But it could be that the way you deliver your advice — rather than the advice itself — could be the cause of a negative reaction. Think about exactly how you approach giving advice and then assess your technique. Here's how: Take the following quiz, based on advice from James Lundy, author of *T.E.A.M.S.: How to Develop Peak Performance Teams for World-Class Results* (Dartnell). Respond **YES** or **NO**:

	YES	NO
1. I check first to see if my co-worker is in a receptive mood for constructive criticism.	☐	☐
2. I plan exactly what I would say to him or her — and how I'd say it — to minimize the chance that they'd take offense.	☐	☐
3. I know for sure that my "delivery style" is not demeaning, patronizing, or sarcastic.	☐	☐
4. I am very specific with my advice, rather than vague or ambiguous.	☐	☐
5. I focus on his or her behavior or actions, rather than on personality or character traits.	☐	☐
6. I tell the recipient why I am offering this advice.	☐	☐
7. Self-interest is not one of my motives; I'm not trying to bring the recipient down a peg or two or get back at him or her in some way.	☐	☐
8. I keep it short, knowing that going on and on would only increase the risk of information overload and defensiveness on his or her part.	☐	☐

DO YOU KNOW HOW TO OFFER ADVICE? If you responded **YES** to most of the above statements, then you're on the right track. They represent everything you did right. Be sure to review the statements to which you responded **NO**, and try to avoid making these mistakes the next time you give constructive criticism.

FEEDBACK VS. CRITICISM

Do you understand the difference between feedback and criticism? Marty Brounstein, author of *Handling the Difficult Employee* (Crisp Publications), defines feedback as "information or input returned to the other person." By contrast, criticism is "the passing of unfavorable judgment, directed at a person." Praise is "the passing of a favorable judgment." See if you can identify the following statements as either **PRAISE, CRITICISM,** or **CONSTRUCTIVE FEEDBACK.**

1. I'm really disappointed with your efforts lately. You know what I mean. _____

2. I want you to understand why that effort with the customer didn't go well. First, the customer's concerns weren't really acknowledged. While you tried to get him to tell you his problem, you didn't express empathy with how he was feeling. Second, he didn't agree with the solution you proposed, and you didn't attempt to explore the reasons why he disagreed. _____

3. You really did a nice job on that last project. You put in some excellent work. _____

4. Your recent extra efforts to help the team have really paid off. You enabled us to maintain our output levels when nearly half the staff was out with the flu. Thanks for going above and beyond the call of duty when we really needed it. _____

5. That presentation you gave wasn't exactly an eye-opener. You were very boring. _____

DO YOU KNOW HOW TO CRAFT FEEDBACK? Here are the proper designations for the above-listed feedback statements: Nos. 1 and 5: **CRITICISM;** Nos. 2 and 4: **CONSTRUCTIVE FEEDBACK;** No. 3: **PRAISE.** If you had a hard time distinguishing which was which, you're probably not offering effective feedback to your teammates and other co-workers. The next time you feel the need to respond to a co-worker's performance, make sure it's the right kind of feedback for that person and that situation. Try to acknowledge the person's efforts (as in the second example above) and offer some helpful, practical details on how he or she could improve the next time around.

'DIFFICULT' PEOPLE CAN BE AN ASSET

Many "difficult" people are smart and creative but just can't adjust to workplace regulations, says author Twyla Dell in *An Honest Day's Work* (Crisp Publications). To see if your "difficult" co-workers have more to offer than you may be giving them credit for, take the following test. Place a check mark after each statement that applies to these nonconformists:

1. They don't like being told what to do. ☐
2. They have ideas on how to organize and run things better. ☐
3. When they aren't challenged, they aren't productive. ☐
4. When they don't see the final results of their work, they become angry or paranoid. ☐
5. They hate being left out of meetings to which they feel they can contribute. ☐
6. They are the first to ask for improved tools or system upgrades. ☐
7. Unless they can see "the big picture," they don't enjoy their work. ☐
8. They want to have a say in every project's final outcome. ☐
9. When they get tired or bored, they use humor to revive themselves. ☐
10. They want training in new skills. ☐
11. When they do good work, they expect recognition. ☐
12. They resent it when people forget their names. ☐
13. They become bored quickly with repetitive work. ☐
14. They prefer variety in their work pace and tasks. ☐

HOW DIFFICULT ARE THEY? While some of these attitudes and actions may seem annoying, each is an attribute of a star team performer. Try giving these people more room to do what they do best, and your whole company may benefit.

EGOS OBSTACLE TO COOPERATION

Strong personalities tend to handle customers rather well, in one-on-one situations. They are usually able to take control of an interaction with an internal or external customer and direct the situation to a positive outcome. Unfortunately, problems sometimes arise when these same co-workers need to work with one another. When they are no longer in complete control of the direction a project takes, their strong egos can become an obstacle to progress.

The following quiz will evaluate how well you deal with difficult teammates, or if you fall under that category yourself. Respond to each question with a **YES** or a **NO**. Then score yourself below:

	YES	NO
1. Do you avoid getting pulled into arguments with aggressive co-workers?	❏	❏
2. Do you acknowledge sarcasm?	❏	❏
3. Do you overreact to criticism?	❏	❏
4. Do you keep calm, even if verbally attacked?	❏	❏
5. Do you arm yourself with facts and data when approaching a "know-it-all"?	❏	❏
6. Do you ask open-ended questions to draw out an unresponsive colleague?	❏	❏
7. Do you consistently disregard others' ideas?	❏	❏
8. Do you avoid gossip about other employees?	❏	❏
9. Do you treat your co-workers with respect?	❏	❏
10. Do you or your colleagues all compete to be leaders, rather than working together?	❏	❏

WHAT'S YOUR SCORE? If you strive toward a cooperative work environment, you should have answered **YES** to Question Nos. 1, 4, 5, 6, 8, and 9 and **NO** to the remainder. Encourage others to take this quiz. Analyze the results, and discuss and highlight how certain behaviors can interfere with the cooperative nature that is imperative to workplace development. However, be careful not to engage in finger-pointing at problem colleagues. You'll get resistance, rather than cooperation, if you push co-workers into a corner.

BE PREPARED WHEN TAKING ON A DIFFICULT CO-WORKER

Do you want to gain more confidence in confronting an intimidating co-worker? Being prepared will make it harder for a difficult colleague to "walk all over" you, says Kathleen Ryan, author of *The Courageous Messenger: How to Successfully Speak Up at Work* (Jossey-Bass). You'll be calm and confident, even if your co-worker does go on the offensive. Take the following quiz to become more at ease with the co-worker you find intimidating. As you fill in each response (with **YES** or **NO**), consider whether it's true or not regarding your last encounter with this person:

	YES	NO
1. I anticipated how she would probably respond — by interrupting or attacking me — when I had my say.	☐	☐
2. I took the time before the encounter to visualize how I could respond if he did get upset.	☐	☐
3. I did role-playing, with a friend or another co-worker playing the part of the "aggressor," to rehearse how I'd react to an offensive response.	☐	☐
4. I practiced my response to my co-worker's anger.	☐	☐
5. I practiced staying cool, calm, and collected in the face of hostility.	☐	☐
6. When my co-worker did begin expressing anger at me, I resisted the impulse to escape the scene.	☐	☐
7. I stood my ground and invited her to tell me more about why she was upset.	☐	☐
8. I listened carefully, so that I could see past his hostile response and act appropriately on that information.	☐	☐

DO YOU KEEP YOUR COOL WITH AN ANGRY CO-WORKER? When you can score eight **YES** answers, you're probably well-prepared for a constructive response in a difficult encounter with your co-worker. It's also helpful to bolster your confidence with self-affirmations, such as "I'm here to build a collaborative relationship, not to be right."

DIPLOMACY TACTICS

Many employers view chronic arguers as troublemakers — no matter how right those employees may be. A reputation as a team player and a diplomat can be invaluable when advancing your career. You don't have to sacrifice your convictions to be affable. The following quiz was designed to show you how. Answer each question **YES** or **NO**; then score yourself:

		YES	NO
1.	Can you avoid discussing volatile topics, such as politics and religion, when having a discussion?	☐	☐
2.	Can you make it clear that some of your thoughts are opinions, not facts?	☐	☐
3.	Do you avoid confrontation with those you're most inclined to argue with?	☐	☐
4.	Do you make certain you hear the other person out before formulating a reply?	☐	☐
5.	Can you find points in the other person's stance you can agree with?	☐	☐
6.	Can you back up your own viewpoints with facts and reasoning, instead of raw emotion?	☐	☐
7.	Do you avoid making sarcastic remarks?	☐	☐
8.	Can you keep your cool when someone tries to goad you?	☐	☐
9.	Do you truly believe that everyone is entitled to their own opinion?	☐	☐
10.	Do you take pride in the near battles that you successfully avoid?	☐	☐

TOTAL NUMBER OF YES ANSWERS _____

HOW DID YOU DO ON THE QUIZ? A score of eight or more **YES** answers indicates that you can be diplomatic. If you're having problems, try to be more tactful.

Since none of these questions asks the impossible, a score of seven or below probably indicates that you place "being right" above teamwork, cooperation, and mutual respect. Standing up for your convictions is one thing, but in the work environment, a strong stance can be interpreted as hindering the team process.

DO YOU GET UP IN ARMS OVER CONFLICT?

Painful as it can be at times, conflict is normal. For healthy relationships at home and at work, we need to be able to approach conflict rationally and then let go of any negative feelings when it's over. No matter how volatile our arguments may become, we can't let them hinder us.

If conflict does disturb you, then perhaps you could benefit from training in conflict management. To find out, take this quiz, which is based on a test designed by Fred Pryor Seminars:

	YES	NO
1. I go out of my way to avoid disagreeing or being in conflict with the majority opinion among my co-workers.	☐	☐
2. I prefer to "give way" to people who are aggressive or disagreeable.	☐	☐
3. I tend to react strongly when I'm upset or challenged.	☐	☐
4. I sometimes take out my anger or frustration on inappropriate "targets" — such as family or friends.	☐	☐
5. When I look back on a conflict I regret, I'm not sure how I could have handled things differently.	☐	☐
6. I don't know how to get others to listen when I speak.	☐	☐
7. I get angry and defensive when I'm criticized.	☐	☐
8. I never stand up to people who try to manipulate or bully me.	☐	☐
9. My conflicts with others keep me from taking an active role in team decision making and problem solving.	☐	☐

TOTAL NUMBER OF YES ANSWERS _____

CAN YOU HANDLE CONFLICT? If you responded **YES** to eight or more of these statements, then your career and relationships could be in jeopardy from misunderstandings and bad feelings. Consider taking a seminar or workshop in conflict management. Ask your supervisor or someone in human resources to recommend a course of action that will help you approach conflict in a more balanced and healthy way.

KEEPING COOL WHEN THINGS GET HOT

A good deal of conflict is caused by tempers that aren't kept in check. When working in close quarters, it is to be expected that stress, differences of opinion and background, and personality clashes can lead to short tempers. However, you can take steps to reduce the occurrence of these conflicts, as well as defuse them when they do arise. Take this quiz, answering **YES** or **NO**, to see how you are doing:

	YES	NO
1. Do you set realistic goals and schedules?	☐	☐
2. Do you expect and accept differences of opinion without taking them personally?	☐	☐
3. Are you able to walk away from a volatile situation when you feel your temper rise?	☐	☐
4. Do you avoid taking out your stress on your teammates?	☐	☐
5. Do you keep team problems in perspective, so they don't get blown out of proportion?	☐	☐
6. Can you usually keep a level head when others around you are losing theirs?	☐	☐
7. Do you know which kinds of situations and people are likely to set you off?	☐	☐
8. Do you avoid these triggers when possible?	☐	☐
9. When team stress follows you home, do you use constructive means, such as exercise, to relieve it?	☐	☐
10. When you do get involved in a conflict, do you stick to logical arguments and avoid emotional ones?	☐	☐

TOTAL NUMBER OF YES ANSWERS _____

HOW'S YOUR TEMPER? A score of eight or more **YES** answers indicates that you are cool as a cucumber most of the time. If you score lower, look at your **NO** responses and strive to turn these areas around. Controlling your temper will help you decrease the number of counterproductive conflicts on your team. But don't expect to eliminate them entirely. Remember, some conflicts are necessary to help your team work out its problems and become more productive.

HOW CAN I REGAIN MY CO-WORKER'S TRUST?

How do you reestablish a co-worker's trust after letting him or her down?

Talk about what happened and how you both feel about it as well as its impact on your ability to work together. If you haven't already admitted you were wrong and apologized, take this opportunity to do so.

To find out more about building trust, take the following quiz. Answer **YES** or **NO** to each question; then check your score below:

	YES	**NO**
1. When you know you've hurt someone's feelings, do you apologize?	☐	☐
2. When you make a mistake that causes inconvenience to others, do you say you're sorry and ask how you can make amends?	☐	☐
3. When a co-worker admits to making a mistake and apologizes to you, do you accept the apology graciously and not hold a grudge?	☐	☐
4. Would you keep it to yourself if a co-worker made a mistake no one else needed to know about?	☐	☐
5. Do you avoid a "What's-in-it-for-me?" approach to the job?	☐	☐
6. Do you act ethically, even when acting unethically is not strictly illegal?	☐	☐
7. Do you generally avoid spreading rumors?	☐	☐
8. When a co-worker entrusts you with a personal or work-related "secret," do you keep that confidence?	☐	☐
9. When you ask people for their input, do you really listen and give them serious consideration?	☐	☐
10. Do you keep your commitments to co-workers?	☐	☐

WHAT'S YOUR SCORE? Nine or more **YES** answers would indicate that you've earned a pretty high level of trust among your co-workers. Eight is average. But if you scored seven or less, you must show others that you are willing to admit to weaknesses and errors — and accept theirs as well. Couple that with working in co-workers' best interests, and you can be assured of their trust.

SHOULD YOU SEND THAT LETTER?

There are serious repercussions to sending letters or memos you've written in the heat of anger. A "hot" letter or memo can never be retracted — and may never be forgiven or forgotten by the recipient. So, before you fire off a letter lambasting your co-worker, go through a step-by-step process. Use the following statements as a guideline. Respond **YES** or **NO** to each; then check your score below:

	YES	NO
1. I've written a rough draft telling my co-worker exactly how hurt I am by her actions.	☐	☐
2. I've destroyed the rough draft, so no one else will see it.	☐	☐
3. I've given myself time to consider whether I really want to write this letter.	☐	☐
4. I've allowed myself time to cool off before drafting a second, more level-headed letter.	☐	☐
5. I've made several drafts to ensure that my letter conveys exactly what I want to say.	☐	☐
6. I've edited out words that could be interpreted as emotional, inflammatory, or accusatory.	☐	☐
7. I've checked the letter for proper grammar, spelling, and sentence structure, knowing that polished writing gives me more credibility.	☐	☐
8. I've focused the content.	☐	☐
9. I've avoided name-calling.	☐	☐
10. I've asked a close, trusted friend to read the letter with an objective eye.	☐	☐

TOTAL NUMBER OF YES ANSWERS _____

WHAT'S YOUR SCORE? Don't send your letter until you can respond **YES** to each statement. Even then, ask yourself, "Do I really want to send this letter?" Send the letter only if you are willing to risk the consequences.

FORMING BOSS – EMPLOYEE RELATIONSHIPS

Establishing a productive work relationship with your direct supervisor requires you to learn about your boss' work style and how best you can blend your own style with his or hers. Aim to establish a strong foundation for a mutually beneficial relationship with your supervisor. Start by answering the following questions **YES** or **NO** to get yourself on the right track:

	YES	NO
1. Do you align your priorities with those of your boss?	☐	☐
2. Do you make sure you understand your boss' directions the first time by asking the right questions?	☐	☐
3. Do you know your boss' expectations for you?	☐	☐
4. Do you keep the boss informed of work-related events that happen in his or her absence?	☐	☐
5. Do you group your work questions together, so that you limit your interruptions?	☐	☐
6. Do you communicate with your boss in the way he or she prefers (e.g., e-mail or voice mail)?	☐	☐
7. Are you honest about the amount and type of work you can handle?	☐	☐
8. Do you alert your boss to problems that may delay deadlines as soon as they arise?	☐	☐
9. Do you keep matters discussed between you and your boss confidential?	☐	☐
10. Do you make sure your boss is aware of your successes?	☐	☐

TOTAL NUMBER OF YES ANSWERS _____

WHAT'S YOUR SCORE? A score of eight or more **YES** answers indicates that you are making a concerted effort to establish a symbiotic working relationship with your boss. By keeping the lines of communication open, you will discover what skills and practices you need to hone in order to become a productive, successful part of this important workplace team.

CREATING BOSS BONDS

Every boss–employee relationship will be somewhat different, depending upon the personalities involved, the organizational culture, and the tasks to be accomplished. However, most good multilevel work bonds exhibit trust, honesty, and a kind of interdependence. To determine where your relationship may be lacking, take the following quiz, responding **TRUE** or **FALSE** to each statement:

	TRUE	FALSE
1. I know that my supervisor will give my new ideas fair and careful consideration.	☐	☐
2. I feel comfortable discussing with my boss personal issues as they relate to my job.	☐	☐
3. I can say "No" to my manager without fear of retribution.	☐	☐
4. I express my opinions freely — even if they contradict my boss' views.	☐	☐
5. I understand my supervisor's motives for his or her actions as they affect the team.	☐	☐
6. I keep my boss informed of project progress — regardless of whether it's smooth or rough going.	☐	☐
7. I meet with my manager regularly on a one-on-one basis, as well as with the rest of my team.	☐	☐
8. I can count on my supervisor for timely, honest, and constructive feedback.	☐	☐
9. The lines of communication go both ways.	☐	☐
10. I respect my boss as an integral member of my work team.	☐	☐

WHAT'S YOUR SCORE? Each of these elements is essential to a good boss–employee relationship, so a response of **TRUE** to each statement is desired. Look at the statements that are **FALSE** for your relationship, and determine what areas need work in your situation. A good start would be to sit down with your supervisor and discuss these areas. He or she can't be expected to respond to your needs without knowing what they are. Understand your role in the relationship as well. You have a duty to be honest and understanding yourself. You'll both need to work to create that bond.

OPEN YOUR MIND TO PEERS' LESSONS

You can learn a lot from your co-workers, no matter what their individual titles may be. You have nothing to lose — and knowledge to gain — by sitting down with your peers and benefiting from their experience and expertise. To get yourself in the right frame of mind, answer the following questions YES or NO:

	YES	NO
1. Do you concede that you can and should learn something from all your colleagues?	❏	❏
2. Do you welcome offers of assistance in a gracious manner?	❏	❏
3. When a co-worker is instructing you, do you give that person your complete attention?	❏	❏
4. Do you take notes, even if it hasn't been suggested?	❏	❏
5. Do you question anything about which you are confused?	❏	❏
6. Do you help your peer instructor by pointing out the areas in which you need the most instruction?	❏	❏
7. Do you repeat your peer's lessons, in your own words, to make sure you understand each other?	❏	❏
8. Do you keep your thoughts, questions, and comments entirely focused on the subject matter at hand?	❏	❏
9. Are you open to new ideas, even if you think you know the answers?	❏	❏
10. Do you offer encouragement and express gratitude to a peer who takes the time to teach you?	❏	❏

TOTAL NUMBER OF YES ANSWERS _____

WHAT'S YOUR SCORE? Each question should have elicited a YES. Any NO response will be a barrier that will prevent you from benefiting completely from your colleagues' knowledge. It's important for peers to share their expertise with one another so that you can approach projects from a common pool of knowledge. Open your mind to what your peers have to offer.

GO FOR 'WIN-WIN' OUTCOME

The underlying element that should guide all negotiation efforts is to strive for a "win-win" outcome. This is especially important in a team-based work environment, where productivity depends upon working together toward a common goal. Take the following quiz, based on one from *Successful Negotiation* (Crisp Publications), to see how you measure up on the negotiating scale:

TRUE FALSE

1. Prior to a negotiation, you can learn much of what you need to know by doing research. ☐ ☐
2. Planning ahead isn't possible in negotiation. ☐ ☐
3. What you expect is directly related to what you get. ☐ ☐
4. Conflict is an important part of negotiation. ☐ ☐
5. Successful negotiators stress winning at any cost. ☐ ☐
6. Weak negotiators use compromise to save face. ☐ ☐
7. Your objectives for every negotiation should be carefully thought out. ☐ ☐
8. Negotiating skills, like most people skills, are something you either have or don't have. ☐ ☐
9. The best negotiators are those with the most authority. ☐ ☐
10. A "post-negotiation analysis" will help with future efforts. ☐ ☐

WHAT'S YOUR SCORE? You should have responded **TRUE** to the following statements: 1, 3, 4, 7, and 10. Here's why the others are **FALSE:** (2) You can plan by learning all you can about the topic and preparing a list of points you want to address and arguments you can use. (5) Winning isn't the point of negotiation — working toward a common goal is the point. (6) True compromise takes more strength of character than either winning or backing down. (8) Knowing how to work effectively with people is a largely learned trait. Any skill can be learned. (9) Too much authority on the part of one of the negotiating parties often leads to an unfair settlement. It's best if all parties operate at the same team level. Negotiation is a powerful team tool. Give it the serious attention it deserves.

RAISING 'DIVERSITY AWARENESS'

It's important to develop "diversity awareness" as a safeguard against possible intolerance or prejudice. To test your diversity awareness, take the following quiz. Respond **YES** or **NO** to each statement to see how you measure up:

	YES	NO
1. You believe that all people deserve to be treated with equal care and respect.	❑	❑
2. You welcome the opportunity to work with and serve people who are different from you — in color, religion, or racial origin.	❑	❑
3. You don't show impatience when talking with someone who has a strong accent or a minimal grasp of English.	❑	❑
4. You don't make assumptions about people based on their race or religion.	❑	❑
5. You never make jokes that others might interpret as racist.	❑	❑
6. If someone else makes a joke that you view as racist, you speak up and voice your distaste.	❑	❑
7. You educate yourself about other cultures.	❑	❑
8. You don't assume that cultural practices are wrong just because they are different from your own.	❑	❑
9. You avoid speaking in a condescending manner to people who are still learning to speak English.	❑	❑
10. You feel comfortable showing interest in and asking questions about other people's social, cultural, and religious traditions and practices.	❑	❑

TOTAL NUMBER OF YES ANSWERS _____

WHAT'S YOUR CULTURAL SENSITIVITY LEVEL? If you responded **YES** to nine or more statements, your diversity awareness is high. If you scored lower, there are areas where you still allow some prejudice to surface in your dealings with others. Work to eliminate these. Encourage co-workers to take this quiz, too. Discuss the results, and look for ways that you can raise diversity awareness throughout your organization.

KNOWING WHEN TO LAUGH

Humor at work can be a great source of energy. It can serve to alleviate the stress in a business situation and enable people to be more open to new ideas, more relaxed, and generally more creative. The following checklist identifies some appropriate ways in which you can use humor in your workplace. Place a check mark next to each way you use humor:

1. To put customers and business contacts at ease. ☐
2. To break the ice when talking with new acquaintances. ☐
3. To boost my co-workers' morale. ☐
4. To form bonds with colleagues, subordinates, and supervisors. ☐
5. To make myself feel better when a day doesn't go as well as I'd like. ☐
6. To help me and my colleagues relax and be creative when solving problems. ☐
7. To lighten the workplace mood and increase my energy. ☐
8. To keep difficult situations in the right perspective. ☐
9. To show that I empathize with others' problems. ☐
10. To help promote cooperation among my co-workers. ☐

HELPFUL HUMOR: The more check marks you have listed above, the better you are at using humor to make your workplace less stressful and more productive. However, humor doesn't always have a place in every work situation. Humor shouldn't be used when it would belittle the ideas or opinions of others; disrupt discussions about serious issues, such as new policies or organizational changes; sidetrack efforts to meet deadlines; or make co-workers uncomfortable by addressing tasteless or controversial topics.

Try using your humor as a catalyst for creativity and productivity. And use your best judgment to determine when your sense of humor could disrupt team efforts and impede your progress toward greater goals.

CHAPTER 4
CUSTOMER RELATIONS
KEEP THEM COMING BACK

*Nothing is ever gained by winning an argument
and losing a customer.*

— C.F. Norton

Your customer service representatives are often times the first people, and sometimes the only people, your customers deal with. Whether on the phone or person-to-person, whether dealing with satisfied or angry customers, whether attracting new customers or retaining current ones, your service representatives must put their best foot forward at all times.

The quizzes in this section are designed to help you and your service representatives evaluate your dedication to quality customer service. Quizzes are structured to enable you to "zero in" on ways to enhance service, keep customers coming back, and troubleshoot some common problems and issues that customer service representatives face.

How does your customer service department rate? Are your service representatives doing everything they can to keep your customers coming back? Have them test their customer savvy by completing quizzes on "Earning Customers' Respect" or "How *Not* to Turn Your Customers Off." Customer retention is an imperative. Your organization's sales and reputation depend on it.

Do your customer service representatives seem at a loss when dealing with hot-headed customers? Use the quiz on "Calming Down an Angry Customer" to help them get a grasp on how to defuse difficult situations and help them maintain high quality service.

With today's increasingly diverse workforce and customer base, are your service representatives making it a priority to be sensitive to customers from different backgrounds and cultures? The quiz "Today's Customers Seem Different" will allow your customer service employees to measure their awareness of cultural differences and to use this insight to better understand their customers.

These are just a few examples quizzes in this chapter that will help your representatives rate themselves or compare their customer relations skills with their peers. Quiz scores reveal the strengths of your service representatives and point out areas they can work on to improve their performance and your bottom line. The commentary included with each quiz provides reinforcement for service representatives that are on the right track and suggestions for those who want to improve in certain areas.

Customer-oriented, sensitive, and responsive representatives are important assets. These quizzes allow you to measure and improve the performance of these valuable employees.

ARE CUSTOMERS PART OF YOUR JOB?

Because many companies have designated customer service departments, others in the workplace often think that's where service ends. In other words, they believe the term *service* applies only to those who deal directly with customers — and think of customer service as "someone else's department." Does your job have anything to do with customer service? Take the following quiz to find out:

	YES	NO
1. Do you ever answer outside telephone lines at work?	☐	☐
2. Does your work affect co-workers who deal directly with customers?	☐	☐
3. Do you have anything to do with creating your company's products?	☐	☐
4. Do you work directly or indirectly with your billing department?	☐	☐
5. Do you take phone messages for co-workers?	☐	☐
6. Does anyone rely on you to produce quality work in a timely fashion?	☐	☐
7. Do you play a part in implementing your company's services?	☐	☐
8. Do you ever meet with or talk to business associates who visit your workplace?	☐	☐
9. Do you generate correspondence sent to people inside or outside the company?	☐	☐
10. Does your outstanding work help others do their jobs more easily?	☐	☐

WHERE ARE YOUR CUSTOMERS? If you answered **YES** to any of the above questions, you play a part in customer service, either inside or outside the organization. What you do affects customers' perceptions of your organization. The point is that everyone in an organization, in some way, ends up serving customers — or co-workers who do. That's a critical point to remember, especially if you think that your job isn't important to your company's overall service efforts.

DEALING WITH TODAY'S CUSTOMERS

Service experts confirm the common perception that today's customers are more demanding — and volatile. All the more reason, then, to learn as much as you can about how to communicate in a way that is most likely to keep customers happy. Take the following quiz to see how well you're able to avoid unintentional gaffes that can offend or antagonize customers. Respond **YES** or **NO** to each statement:

	YES	NO
1. I never belittle customers' concerns.	☐	☐
2. I don't imply that customers don't have a right to their emotions.	☐	☐
3. I avoid telling customers what they should or shouldn't do.	☐	☐
4. I don't ask "why" questions ("Why did you ...?") because they tend to make customers defensive.	☐	☐
5. I never say "I can't," knowing that customers interpret this as "I won't."	☐	☐
6. I don't use jargon or buzzwords that customers may not understand.	☐	☐
7. I avoid using the word "policy," because it turns off most customers.	☐	☐
8. I learn how to pronounce customers' names correctly.	☐	☐
9. I don't swear in front of customers, or use racist or sexist terms.	☐	☐
10. I'm careful about how I express humor with customers, never telling a joke that some people may find offensive.	☐	☐

TOTAL NUMBER OF YES ANSWERS _____

HOW DO YOU RATE? If you scored at least nine **YES** answers, you appear to be doing many things that should help keep customers satisfied. Keep in mind that — despite all your good efforts — some customers just seem to have been *born* cranky. The good news is that these difficult customers will soon be walking out the door — and you'll be dealing with others who will be more appreciative of your goodwill and service.

EARNING CUSTOMERS' RESPECT

Do you know how to gain and retain the respect of customers?
Those of us who serve customers take our turn at being customers when we shop, do our banking, have our cars serviced, and so on. So think in terms of what you find most appealing in service providers. Once you've identified these qualities, you'll know what to do to appeal to customers. Respond **YES** or **NO** to the following statements to help you identify what you're doing right, right now:

	YES	NO
1. I greet each customer with a sincere smile and a warm welcome — even when I'm having a bad day.	☐	☐
2. I never make light of a customer's concern or complaint.	☐	☐
3. I'm knowledgeable enough about my company and its products and services to answer customer questions.	☐	☐
4. If I can't answer questions on the spot, I know where to find the answers.	☐	☐
5. I never give customers the impression that it's too much trouble to give them a little extra help.	☐	☐
6. I watch my language around customers.	☐	☐
7. I admit my mistakes and offer to make things right.	☐	☐
8. I treat all customers with respect and care.	☐	☐
9. I'm not afraid to ask customers, "Is everything OK?"	☐	☐
10. I never show impatience with or try to rush customers.	☐	☐
11. I never let a customer comment or complaint go by without making a positive and empathetic response.	☐	☐
12. I make good eye contact with customers at least once or twice during a transaction — and as I greet and say goodbye to them.	☐	☐

TOTAL NUMBER OF YES ANSWERS _____

WHAT'S YOUR "RESPECT" RATE? If you responded **YES** to 11 or more of the above statements, you're already doing many of the things guaranteed to make customers like and respect you.

TODAY'S CUSTOMERS SEEM DIFFERENT

Many companies are experiencing a growth in the cultural diversity of their work force. Experts predict that women and minorities will dominate tomorrow's workforce. Also, we've moved into a global economy in recent years. So, it should come as no surprise that your customers seem different. Your attitude plays a key role in how effectively you deal with them. Evaluate your present attitudes toward those you see as "different" by answering these questions:

	YES	NO
1. Can you deal effectively with people from other backgrounds?	☐	☐
2. Do you try to avoid offending those whom you regard as different?	☐	☐
3. Do you avoid generalizing about customers based on their race or ethnic background?	☐	☐
4. Can you cooperate with those who speak and act differently?	☐	☐
5. Do you try to treat all your customers fairly?	☐	☐
6. Are you aware that certain cultural customs are merely different, not wrong?	☐	☐
7. No matter what form it takes, are you intolerant of prejudice?	☐	☐
8. Do you avoid judging others' behaviors by comparing them with your own?	☐	☐
9. Are you aware that some ethnic groups conduct business in different ways?	☐	☐
10. Are you patient and flexible when dealing with customers who seem "different"?	☐	☐

TOTAL NUMBER OF YES ANSWERS _____

WHAT'S YOUR SCORE? In a culturally varied business community, it's essential that you answer **YES** to each of the above questions. Any **NO** responses have the potential to cause you problems. Strive to eliminate them. Remember that adaptability and an open mind are your best allies. Your professional success depends on them.

DO YOU KNOW YOUR CUSTOMERS?

Famous trial attorney Melvin Belli asserts, "There is no such thing as having too much information." His statement applies equally to customer service. You can never have too much information about your customers. Information enables you to know how your customers think about your products and services, your company, and your competition. Then, you are equipped to serve their needs. Take this quiz to see how well you know your customers:

	YES	NO
1. I have all pertinent information on each customer written down.	☐	☐
2. I know the key decision makers in each account.	☐	☐
3. I know something about the likes and dislikes of each customer.	☐	☐
4. I know my competitors' situations with each account.	☐	☐
5. I know the purchasing history of my products with each customer.	☐	☐
6. I know the problems that have occurred with each account, when and why they occurred, and how they were resolved.	☐	☐
7. I know how buying decisions are made at my customers' companies.	☐	☐
8. I know the major buying determinants (service, price, quality) with each account.	☐	☐
9. I know each customer's plans for growth and diversification.	☐	☐
10. I'm familiar with the level of technical knowledge and expertise of my customers.	☐	☐

YOUR SCORE: You should have responded **YES** to each of these statements if you really know your customers. Review your **NO** responses and gather the information you need to change them to a **YES**. There's no need to hint or hunt around for the answers. Come right out and tell your customers that you want to get to know them better so that you can better serve their needs.

IS IT EVER OK TO BE RUDE?

It's never OK to be rude to a customer. Even if you're feeling stressed or emotional, or the customer is being unreasonable, there's always an alternative to rudeness. Answer **YES** or **NO** to the following questions to determine your own courtesy quotient:

	YES	NO
1. Are you aware of it when you're in a bad mood ?	☐	☐
2. Do you avoid revealing your bad mood to customers?	☐	☐
3. Are you extra careful to remain cool, calm, and polite when you're feeling anything but that way?	☐	☐
4. Do you consistently acknowledge customers with a smile and a friendly greeting?	☐	☐
5. When you just can't satisfy a customer, do you excuse yourself courteously and ask your supervisor to help?	☐	☐
6. Do you seek assistance from a co-worker before you reach the "boiling point"?	☐	☐
7. Do you try to model your own service manner after that of someone whose customer skills you admire?	☐	☐
8. Do you believe good manners are the essence of good business?	☐	☐
9. Do you consider "please" and "thank you" crucial, rather than old-fashioned courtesies?	☐	☐
10. Do you believe that leaving a customer feeling hurt, unhappy, or dissatisfied is the worst service blunder you can make?	☐	☐

TOTAL NUMBER OF YES ANSWERS _____

WHAT'S YOUR COURTESY QUOTIENT? You rate an excellent if you scored at least nine **YES** answers. If your score is lower, take the time to review these questions. Even though you may be committed to courtesy, it may not always be evident in your daily customer interactions. Remember, consistency of mood and attitude is most important in service. Treating people well, or not, according to your whim of the moment isn't what service excellence is all about. Consistently treating them well will make you stand out.

HOW *NOT* TO TURN YOUR CUSTOMERS OFF

Certainly customers like friendly service from people unafraid to reveal their human side. But you need to make sure your friendly service doesn't become too informal or go too far and become obtrusive. After all, this is a business relationship you have — or are trying to establish — with the customer. Your encounter can be sociable, but this is not a social occasion.

If you know the customer well enough, it's OK to ask, "How did your son's graduation go?" But it's not appropriate to take up the customer's time bragging at length about your own kids, Bart Breighner, author of *Face to Face Selling* (JIST Works), says. It's the kind of thing that can irritate customers to the point where they don't come back.

To find out what you might be doing to turn customers off, take the following quiz based in part on material in Breighner's book.

Check the **DO** or **DON'T** column for each statement:

	DO	DON'T
1. I interrupt when the customer is talking.	☐	☐
2. I smile and laugh a lot to keep it light.	☐	☐
3. I chew gum to keep my breath sweet.	☐	☐
4. I share rumors that will interest customers.	☐	☐
5. I criticize co-workers or other customers.	☐	☐
6. I use first names when I meet people.	☐	☐
7. I tell off-color jokes to some customers.	☐	☐
8. I show irritation if someone deserves it.	☐	☐
9. I maintain constant eye contact.	☐	☐
10. I talk about myself and my preferences.	☐	☐
11. I give flip answers when customers ask dumb questions.	☐	☐

HOW DO YOU RELATE TO CUSTOMERS? If you checked the **DON'T** column for each of these statements, you need not worry about alienating customers with annoying habits. But check your "performance" occasionally just to make sure. After the next customer encounter, for instance, take this quiz again to see if you've met your own high standards.

WHAT IMPRESSIONS DO YOU MAKE?

Sometimes, customers are not easy to read. It's not always apparent how they feel about the service you are providing. Nonetheless, customers' opinions of the people who serve them can make all the difference to a company's overall success or failure. Do your customers like what they get from you? Take the following quiz to find out:

	YES	NO
1. Do you find that even fierce customers respond favorably to your patience and courtesy?	☐	☐
2. Do customers ask for you by name or seek you out personally to do business?	☐	☐
3. Do customers with problems leave with clear, understandable solutions?	☐	☐
4. When you smile and chat with customers, do they respond in the same way?	☐	☐
5. Are customers unaware when your mood is down?	☐	☐
6. Do customers ever seem surprised by the high level of service they receive from you?	☐	☐
7. Do new customers ever tell you that you've been recommended by another customer?	☐	☐
8. Do customers know that their concerns are your top priority?	☐	☐
9. Are quiet customers comfortable bringing returned merchandise or a problem to you?	☐	☐
10. Do those customers seem relieved and pleased when they don't get the "third degree" from you?	☐	☐

TOTAL NUMBER OF YES ANSWERS _____

WHAT DO YOUR CUSTOMERS THINK OF YOU? A score of eight or more **YES** answers is a sign that your customers appreciate your efforts — and they return to do business because of that. A lower score indicates that customers aren't knocked out by the service you give. Review those questions to which you answered **NO** and work on improving your performance in those areas. Be aware of the indications — both subtle and obvious — that customers use to express their levels of comfort and satisfaction with your service.

DON'T COURTESY ACTIONS SPEAK LOUDER THAN WORDS?

Being courteous is a way of smoothing out all the rough spots of our daily contacts with others. A rep may go out of his or her way to serve customers efficiently, but, without using courteous language, those good actions may quickly go unnoticed. Courteous language isn't just an extra; it's a basic component of quality service. Check your own level of politeness with this quiz.

How often do you use the following phrases?

		NEVER	SOMETIMES	ALWAYS
1.	"Please"	☐	☐	☐
2.	"Thank you"	☐	☐	☐
3.	The customer's name	☐	☐	☐
4.	"I'm very sorry."	☐	☐	☐
5.	"Excuse me."	☐	☐	☐
6.	Friendly greetings, like "Hello" and "Goodbye"	☐	☐	☐
7.	"You're welcome."	☐	☐	☐
8.	"We appreciate your business."	☐	☐	☐
9.	"I'd be happy to do that for you."	☐	☐	☐
10.	"May I help you please?"	☐	☐	☐
11.	"I'm sorry to keep you waiting."	☐	☐	☐
12.	"Thank you for calling."	☐	☐	☐
13.	"It's been a pleasure serving you."	☐	☐	☐

DO YOU GIVE COURTESY ITS DUE? Give yourself 10 points for each phrase you use **ALWAYS**; seven points for those you use **SOMETIMES**; and no points for those you use **NEVER**. If your points total 124–130, congratulations! You're a true service professional. You give customers fast, efficient, courteous service backed with the appropriate words and behaviors. A score of 115–123 shows you generally are courteous but need to begin incorporating more courtesy phrases into your conversation. Any lower score indicates that you are falling short in expressing a courteous attitude to customers. No matter how well you treat customers, you may not be serving them politely. Make it a point to use more of these phrases.

HOW TO BUILD CUSTOMER LOYALTY

Every customer service rep can help build customer loyalty. The following quiz can show you how. Answer each question **YES** or **NO**; then check your score below:

		YES	NO
1.	Do you send letters or e-mail messages, thanking customers for their business?	☐	☐
2.	Do you fax customers information about discounts or sales in which they might be interested?	☐	☐
3.	Do you give your best customers a telephone number where they can reach you directly?	☐	☐
4.	Have you given customers your pager number, so they can reach you in an emergency?	☐	☐
5.	Do you call customers just to say "Hello" and inquire about the quality of the service they've received?	☐	☐
6.	Have you considered offering training videos or audiotapes to help customers get the most from your products?	☐	☐
7.	Do you keep track of customer questions or concerns?	☐	☐
8.	Do you visit customer sites, so you can better understand how your services can meet their needs?	☐	☐
9.	Do you make it easy for customers to maneuver their way through your phone system?	☐	☐
10.	Do you always let customers know how much you appreciate their business?	☐	☐

TOTAL NUMBER OF YES ANSWERS _____

HOW WELL DO YOU BUILD LOYALTY? Give yourself 10 points for every **YES** answer. A score of 90–100 shows that you are making a conscious effort to turn your regular customers into loyal, repeat customers. A score of 80 is average, but if you scored lower, try to begin implementing the ideas outlined in this quiz. *Remember:* You have the power to make customer encounters magical and memorable — and to keep customers coming back.

CALMING DOWN AN ANGRY CUSTOMER

How do you relieve or moderate a customer's anger and focus the heat away from yourself? How do you help the customer understand that you agree with his or her feelings and still be able to offer a solution? Answer **TRUE** or **FALSE** in response to the following statements to indicate if they will help you calm down an angry customer, overcome the objection, and complete the sale:

	TRUE	FALSE
1. I understand most of your concerns.	☐	☐
2. I know that price is important to your boss.	☐	☐
3. Once you have had time to think it over, call me.	☐	☐
4. I will send you more information immediately.	☐	☐
5. Aren't you glad I made you aware of that?	☐	☐
6. I appreciate your feelings about the issue.	☐	☐
7. I respect your position.	☐	☐

ANSWERS: STATEMENT NO. 1: FALSE. This response may make the customer feel as though you don't agree with the details most important to him or her. A better reply would be, "I understand your concerns."

STATEMENT NO. 2: FALSE. A reference to the customer's superior may make the matter worse. Try, "I know that price is important to you."

STATEMENT NO. 3: FALSE. If you leave before you settle the issue or agree to the next step, the customer may never call you. Agree with the customer by saying, "Of course you need to think it over. Let's get together early next week to resolve the issue."

STATEMENT NO. 4: TRUE. You may feel that the customer doesn't have all the information needed to make a buying decision. This response implies that the customer will want to know more. It's important to follow up promptly if the meeting ends at this stage.

STATEMENT NO. 5: FALSE. If the customer raises an objection, he or she is not happy about the information. A more professional reply would be, "I'm sorry that data upset you. Tell me why the information causes you to react that way."

STATEMENT NO. 6: TRUE. This is a simple response that merely offers agreement.

STATEMENT NO. 7: TRUE. This reply will help defuse the situation, as long as you sincerely feel that way.

RETAINING CUSTOMER LOYALTY

Retaining the customers you have is a sound business strategy, emphasizes Barbara Glanz, co-author, of *Building Customer Loyalty* (Irwin). Glanz cites a *Harvard Business Review* article: "As a customer's relationship with the company lengthens, profits rise. Companies can boost profits by almost 100 percent by retaining just 5 percent more of their customers." Proof positive that working to build customer loyalty is worthwhile. Are you doing what it takes to earn and build customer loyalty? Take the following self-assessment exercise — based on one offered in Glanz's book — to find out. Respond **ALMOST ALWAYS (AA), SOMETIMES (S)**, or **ALMOST NEVER (N)** to each statement:

1. I know my company's products and services well, and I'm committed to helping my customers learn about them. _____

2. I offer customers options and alternatives to help them make wise buying decisions. _____

3. I do whatever it takes to meet customer needs. _____

4. I take personal responsibility for solving customer problems. _____

5. I learn my customers' names, use them at least once during the transaction — and remember them. _____

6. I treat my customers with the kind of respect that says, "I trust and believe you." _____

7. I thank customers for choosing to do business with our organization. _____

8. I empathize with customers' concerns, even if I don't agree with them. _____

9. I keep my promises — such as returning customers' calls within 24 hours. _____

10. I stay calm and treat customers courteously, even when constant interruptions and demands make my workday chaotic. _____

DO YOU HAVE WHAT IT TAKES? If you answered **ALMOST ALWAYS** to nine or more of the statements, you're well aware of what it takes to build customer loyalty, and you're acting on this knowledge. Occasionally, review this quiz to make sure you keep doing all the right things.

DO ALL CUSTOMERS DESERVE EQUAL TREATMENT?

Every customer deserves superior customer service. But long-term customers deserve extra attention. For one thing, it's important not to take them for granted. Don't assume that, because they have bought from you in the past, they will continue to do so in the future. In his book *Great Customer Service for Your Small Business* (Crisp), Clearwater, Florida–based consultant Richard Gerson lists several tips for retaining long-term customers. The following questions are based on his ideas. Answer **YES** or **NO** to each to see how you treat your long-term customers:

	YES	NO
1. Do you call customers by their names?	☐	☐
2. Do you focus on what customers are saying to you?	☐	☐
3. Are you concerned about each customer as an individual?	☐	☐
4. Are you courteous to customers?	☐	☐
5. Are you responsive to the needs of individual customers?	☐	☐
6. Do you make it a point of knowing your customers' personal buying histories and motivations?	☐	☐
7. Do you spend as much time as necessary with each customer to be sure his or her needs have been met?	☐	☐
8. Do you involve customers in your business by asking for their advice and suggestions?	☐	☐
9. Do you try to make each customer feel important?	☐	☐
10. Do you listen in order to understand customers, and then speak to them in terms they understand?	☐	☐

TOTAL NUMBER OF YES ANSWERS _____

HOW DO YOU TREAT LONG-TERM CUSTOMERS? If you answered **YES** to nine or more questions, you're probably giving long-term customers the extra care they deserve. Eight **YES** answers is average. But if your score was seven or less, refocus your attention on customers you deal with regularly. Try to find ways to let them know you think they're special.

MEETING CUSTOMERS' EXPECTATIONS

"To touch base with key customer expectations, review your company's or team's service mission. Then, try to determine if your service interactions support this mission," says trainer Brian Taylor. He explains that service people at the Cleveland Service Center of New York Life Insurance Co. routinely ask themselves key questions. Specifically, they check to see if they're fulfilling the company's mission to supply "fast, accurate, knowledgeable, and courteous service." Take the following quiz to determine your ability to deliver on expectations that are common to most customers. Answer each question **YES** or **NO**:

	YES	NO
1. Do you keep callers on hold only very briefly?	☐	☐
2. Do you listen closely to clue in quickly on callers' problems or concerns?	☐	☐
3. When you tell a customer you'll get back to him or her at a certain time, do you keep your promise?	☐	☐
4. Do you go all out to meet any extra needs a customer may have?	☐	☐
5. Are you thoroughly familiar with your company's products or services?	☐	☐
6. Do you know where to find information your customers may need?	☐	☐
7. Are you patient and respectful with upset or difficult customers?	☐	☐
8. Do you apologize when you make mistakes that affect customers?	☐	☐
9. Even when a customer's question implies something negative about your company's products or services, do you answer willingly, rather than defensively?	☐	☐

TOTAL NUMBER OF YES ANSWERS _____

ARE YOU MEETING CUSTOMERS' EXPECTATIONS? If you scored at least eight **YES** answers, you're meeting several key customer expectations. Above all, Taylor emphasizes, you must treat customers "as individuals worthy of your complete attention if you want them to feel good about doing business with you and your company."

TRACK CUSTOMERS' CHANGING NEEDS

Paying attention to customers' changing needs is an excellent way to show that you care about serving their needs — and a great way to increase business. The following quiz shows some ways to put this idea into action. Answer each question **YES** or **NO**:

		YES	NO
1.	Do you try asking customers if their needs have changed in any way?	☐	☐
2.	Do you keep an eye on new trends that relate to the products or services your company offers?	☐	☐
3.	Do you read newspapers and trade publications that serve industries with which your company does business?	☐	☐
4.	Are you conscious of how the various seasons may affect your customers' needs?	☐	☐
5.	When customers report a change of address, do you consider how that may reflect a change in their needs?	☐	☐
6.	Do you try to arrange visits to your customers, so you can determine their needs firsthand?	☐	☐
7.	Do you ask customers if they have friends or family members who could benefit from your services?	☐	☐
8.	If a customer's business is expanding, do you recognize that he or she may need more of your services?	☐	☐
9.	Do you look for new ways to serve customers who have been promoted or have new jobs?	☐	☐
10.	Do you compare a customer's current order with a previous order to gauge changing needs?	☐	☐

TOTAL NUMBER OF YES ANSWERS _____

WHAT'S YOUR SCORE? The more questions you answered **YES**, the more attuned you are to your customers. *Remember*: The ability to identify customers' needs and match products or services to those needs improves service, as well as increases customer satisfaction.

KEEPING YOUR CLIENTS

Keeping your customers happy is one surefire way to get them to return to you. The best customer service reps have a primary goal at work: They want to assist clients politely and efficiently, so everyone benefits. Here's a test to see if you are doing all you can to get your clients to return to you for continued business:

	YES	NO
1. Do you periodically ask clients what they expect from your company?	☐	☐
2. Do you show every customer and co-worker courtesy and respect — no matter what?	☐	☐
3. Do you take the time to understand as much as you can about how your company works?	☐	☐
4. Do you always try to deal with complaints immediately?	☐	☐
5. Do you slightly overestimate how long a service or delivery will take, to allow for the unexpected?	☐	☐
6. Do you make a habit of looking for ways to improve the quality of service you provide?	☐	☐
7. Do you keep records on how you serve your customers?	☐	☐
8. Do you file "feel-good" letters that have complimented you on a job well done?	☐	☐
9. Do you work to satisfy customers' needs, not just to sell them product?	☐	☐
10. Do you follow up with customers to see how your organization is faring with them?	☐	☐

TOTAL NUMBER OF YES ANSWERS _____

DO YOU KNOW HOW TO KEEP CUSTOMERS? Ideally, you should have all **YES** answers to this test. If you scored fewer than eight **YES** answers, keep this test on your desk for a few weeks as a guide. Use the above listed questions to identify your weak spots. Even if your score was satisfactory, this checklist can help remind you to keep up on this vital customer service element. It can also prompt you to explore new ways of improving customer service. Remember that personalized, polite attention is the quickest way to a customer's heart.

WHAT CUSTOMERS
DO AND DON'T WANT

Customer service reps should know as much about their customers' companies as possible. This will help reps determine what customers want and need, as well as what they *don't* want and need. To find out how well you know your customers, respond **TRUE** or **FALSE** to the following statements:

	TRUE	FALSE
1. My customers expect me to give them preferential treatment.	☐	☐
2. My customers appreciate that I do not waste their time with incessant chatter whenever we meet.	☐	☐
3. My customers would not like it if I gossiped about their competitors.	☐	☐
4. My customers expect me to return their phone calls in a timely manner.	☐	☐
5. My customers expect me to be knowledgeable about the products and services my company provides.	☐	☐
6. My customers know I try to resolve their problems as quickly as possible.	☐	☐
7. My customers do not mind if I call them for no reason.	☐	☐
8. My customers expect me to follow up after I've resolved a problem for them or they've purchased a new product.	☐	☐
9. My customers disapprove of my low-key approach.	☐	☐
10. My customers appreciate that I always prepare before talking with them.	☐	☐

DO YOU KNOW YOUR CUSTOMERS? Statement Nos. 2, 3, 4, 5, 6, 8, and 10 are **TRUE**. Statement Nos. 1, 7, and 9 are **FALSE**. Here's why: (1) Most customers don't expect preferential treatment. They just want you to try your best to meet their needs. Beware of customers who constantly expect favors. (7) Most customers prefer you call with a specific purpose in mind. (9) Most customers don't like aggressive, pushy reps. They want to work with professional reps who know what their customers need.

SELF-CONFIDENCE TRANSLATES TO CUSTOMER SERVICE

Self-confidence is the hallmark of the successful customer service rep. After all, if you don't have confidence in yourself, how can you expect anyone else — especially customers — to put faith in you? Does your self-image need some nourishing? To help you find out, use this quiz based on Norman King's confidence tips in *The First Five Minutes* (Prentice Hall). Answer each question **YES** or **NO**; then score yourself below.

		YES	NO
1.	Do you recognize your limitations so you can set goals that are within your reach?	☐	☐
2.	Do you "let yourself off the guilt hook" when you stumble toward achieving a goal?	☐	☐
3.	Do you avoid dwelling on negative incidents from the past?	☐	☐
4.	Do you realize most setbacks are due to outside forces — and aren't your fault?	☐	☐
5.	Are you as tolerant of your mistakes as you are of your customers' errors?	☐	☐
6.	Do you avoid taking personal attacks from callers to heart?	☐	☐
7.	Do you learn from errors you make on the job?	☐	☐
8.	Do you constantly evaluate your progress toward reaching your goals?	☐	☐
9.	Do you pat yourself on the back now and then?	☐	☐
10.	Do you take time to relax and enjoy life?	☐	☐

TOTAL NUMBER OF YES ANSWERS _____

YOUR SELF-CONFIDENCE SCORE: If nine to 10 of your answers are **YES**, good job! You have a healthy level of self-confidence that is no doubt reflected in your work. Eight is average. But if you scored lower, you need to build your confidence. Follow the suggestions in each question. "Be tolerant" of your failures, suggests King, and "set your goals toward ambitions you really want to achieve." At the end of the day, put work out of your mind, and spend time focusing on yourself.

REGULAR 'SELF-REVIEW' GUARANTEES STEADY IMPROVEMENT

The following quiz will help you get ready for a performance review. But, remember, your on-the-job progress should be regular and steady. Make sure you don't simply wait until your review time to take a serious look at your performance. We suggest you take this quiz every month or so to review your ongoing development. With **7** as the highest level of agreement and **1** as the lowest, circle the number that best describes you for each statement:

		AGREE						DISAGREE
1.	I listen attentively when customers speak to me about their problems and needs.	7	6	5	4	3	2	1
2.	I speak in terms customers understand.	7	6	5	4	3	2	1
3.	I try my best, in both my tone of voice and my choice of words, to sound pleasant at all times.	7	6	5	4	3	2	1
4.	I treat customers in a friendly manner.	7	6	5	4	3	2	1
5.	I try not to let angry customers get the best of me.	7	6	5	4	3	2	1
6.	I let unhappy customers know I am sorry they've experienced a problem.	7	6	5	4	3	2	1
7.	When there is a complaint, I try to negotiate a solution that is satisfying to the customer and meets our company's policies.	7	6	5	4	3	2	1
8.	On the telephone I am courteous and avoid putting customers on hold.	7	6	5	4	3	2	1
9.	I make it a point to follow through on my promises to customers.	7	6	5	4	3	2	1
10.	I try to convey to customers the pleasure I feel in serving them.	7	6	5	4	3	2	1

DID YOU PASS YOUR CUSTOMER SERVICE "CHECKUP"? A score of 60–70 indicates that you have an excellent grasp of the skills needed to make every interaction with customers a success. A score of 45–59 is acceptable, but you should look for areas where you scored **3** or lower and try to improve in those particular skills.

CHAPTER 5
TELEPHONE SKILLS

USING THIS POWERFUL COMMUNICATION TOOL
FOR DAILY SUCCESS

What do just about all employees, regardless of status or function, have in common? Answer: They all spend a lot of time on the telephone.

Because much of that telephone time is spent talking with customers, training your employees on basic skills, phone etiquette, and handling tough calls is a necessity. Monitoring performance and providing refresher training sessions are well worth the time they take because the payback is satisfied customers who praise your people for their courtesy and service and provide your organization with repeat business.

How do your employees' telephone skills rate?

Customers tend to have more faith in a company whose employees have a positive attitude and a genuine desire to provide the best service possible. When callers want information or service, are your employees enthusiastic about providing it? Use the quiz "Phone Rep, I Like Your Attitude" to give employees a chance to review the image they present to their customers. Use the results to target areas for improvement.

Do your employees provide enough information in their messages when requesting a return call? Are they clear enough to encourage call-backs? Make sure your employees don't unknowingly turn away customers with their phone messages. Have employees rate their message-leaving skills with the quiz "How Rude! People Don't Return Calls."

Can your employees give a simple answer to a caller's question? Can they supply information without using buzzwords or technical terminology that can confuse, embarrass, or alienate? Use the quiz "Watch Your Language!" to let your employees evaluate whether they are in touch with callers' needs and how skilled they are at communicating on an appropriate level with the customer.

Giving your employees the information and resources they need and training them to treat phone calls as carefully as they handle face-to-face interactions will increase your business. The quizzes are a simple, inexpensive, and easy-to-use tool that will enable you to quickly key into areas that need to be improved, and, at the same time, show your employees where they can enhance their performance.

IT'S NOT A PHONE CALL — IT'S A MEETING!

There's nothing wrong with a little friendliness. But be concerned that friendly chatter doesn't keep you too long from other duties or calls. One of the most effective ways of controlling phone time is to plan calls the way you plan meetings — with a predetermined goal, an agenda, and a specific time frame. The following quiz can help you start planning your phone time. After each statement, rate yourself on the following scale.

SELDOM	SOMETIMES	ALMOST ALWAYS
1	2	3

When it comes to making calls:

1. In advance, I prepare a one-sentence goal for what I expect to accomplish. _____

2. I also make a mental note as to how long I can allow myself to spend on the call. _____

3. I spell out my goal early in the conversation ("Sara, I'm calling to discuss ..."). _____

4. I keep my eye on the clock and stick to the time frame I've allocated for the call. _____

5. I take notes to keep the call focused. _____

6. When conversation veers off track, I pull it back on course. _____

7. Once the topic's been covered, I summarize the main points. _____

8. I ask questions to clarify information if necessary. _____

9. If I want to chat further, I set up time to get together for lunch or to talk on my own time. _____

10. I don't become so obsessed about time that I forget to be courteous to the other party. _____

YOUR TOTAL SCORE _____

YOUR SCORE: A score of 27–30 means you're doing an excellent job controlling your phone time. Twenty–26 is fair; but if your point total was any lower, you need to start planning what you want to accomplish and how much time you can spend talking — before you make your next call.

HOW RUDE!
PEOPLE DON'T RETURN CALLS

Have you noticed that people are not calling you back after you have left several messages asking them to do so?

Before assuming that an epidemic of discourtesy is the reason your phone calls are not being returned, consider the possibility that your messages are not providing enough information or that they're not clear enough to encourage callbacks. To see if that's the case, take the following quiz. Answer each question **YES** or **NO**; then score yourself below.

	YES	NO
1. When I leave a message, I state clearly that I would like the customer to call me back.	☐	☐
2. On messages, I provide my name and spell it out.	☐	☐
3. I always state a purpose for my call.	☐	☐
4. I include my phone number.	☐	☐
5. I indicate the best times for reaching me.	☐	☐
6. I state a time when I will call back if the customer can't reach me.	☐	☐
7. If I need a specific question answered, I include that in my message.	☐	☐
8. I stress the importance of my call.	☐	☐
9. I try not to request a callback if it is not necessary.	☐	☐
10. I try to be available for return calls when I say I will.	☐	☐
11. I include the name of someone else the customer can ask for if I am not available when they call back.	☐	☐
12. When customers do call me back, I let them know I appreciate it.	☐	☐

TOTAL NUMBER OF YES ANSWERS _____

SCORE YOURSELF: If you answered **YES** to 11 or 12 questions, you are leaving thorough messages that encourage customers to return your calls. Nine or 10 is acceptable, but try using the suggestions you overlooked. A score of eight or fewer indicates that customers need more information from you so they'll know how to reach you — and why they should. Use the above suggestions to revamp your phone-message style.

COMMUNICATION CRITICAL
TO PROBLEM-SOLVING PROCESS

There's more to handling a customer's problem than just correcting it. Failure to follow up, for example, may very well negate the goodwill you've generated by handling the problem promptly and efficiently. The following quiz may offer you some insights into the many aspects involved in handling such situations. It is based on the First National Bank of Chicago's "10 Customer Service Commandments":

		YES	NO
1.	Do you call customers back when promised?	☐	☐
2.	When a customer has experienced a problem, do you clearly explain the cause of the difficulty?	☐	☐
3.	Do you make sure callers know the names and numbers of the people they should speak with about their problem?	☐	☐
4.	Do you promptly let the customer know when a problem has been corrected?	☐	☐
5.	Do you allow unhappy customers to speak to someone in authority when they ask?	☐	☐
6.	Do you give customers an idea of how long it will take to resolve a problem?	☐	☐
7.	Do you offer useful alternatives if the problem cannot be resolved exactly as the customer would like?	☐	☐
8.	Do you treat customers like people — not numbers?	☐	☐
9.	Do you tell customers how to avoid future problems?	☐	☐
10.	Do you provide progress reports to the customer if the problem can't be solved immediately?	☐	☐

TOTAL NUMBER OF YES ANSWERS _____

DO YOU FOLLOW THE SERVICE COMMANDMENTS? If you answered 10 questions **YES**, you're doing an excellent job communicating with customers. Nine is average, but if you answered eight or fewer **YES**, you need to direct more attention on your customers' needs. Customers feel better about the outcome if you treat them like partners in the problem-solving process.

DOES STRESS STIFLE THE RIGHT WORDS?

Responding in pressure situations is difficult, but the more experience you have, the easier it becomes. Another way to improve is by memorizing specific answers that work in particular situations and then tailoring them to your unique circumstances. The following quiz can help you rate how well you do now in tough situations. Choose the best response in each scenario, then check your score below. Select **(A), (B),** or **(C)** for each:

1. When a caller with a complaint becomes abusive, you:
   - (a) Give it right back to him in no uncertain terms.
   - (b) Laugh nervously and hang up.
   - (c) Remain calm and say, "I know you're upset, but I can't help you when you're talking this way."

2. Your company has changed some key policies. A customer calls griping, "I liked it the old way!" You:
   - (a) Tell her, "Tough."
   - (b) Explain that the best way to protest would be to take her business elsewhere.
   - (c) Say, "When you've had a chance to try the new system would you complete a comment card? We'd value your opinion."

3. Prices have gone up. A customer complains. You:
   - (a) Ask him, "Aren't we worth it?"
   - (b) Offer him merchandise at the old prices.
   - (c) Say, "I can understand how frustrating it is when prices increase. That's why we've worked so hard to avoid it." Then go on to explain *why* prices have increased.

ARE YOU READY FOR THOSE TOUGH CALLERS? The correct answer in each situation is **(C).** If you missed any, study the correct answer and try to understand why it is preferred. Make a note of those situations in which each response would apply. Then begin tailoring your responses in a similar way.

It might help you to write down some of the key points you need to make in these situations and post it in your work area.

I'VE MADE PROBLEMS WORSE BY HELPING CUSTOMERS

Boston-based consultant Debra J. MacNeil has devised a "Five-Star Approach" to problem resolution, which she describes in her book *Customer Service Excellence* (Business One Irwin). Each point on the star represents one step — acknowledging the problem, assessing the situation, affirming your understanding, analyzing alternatives, and agreeing on a plan of action. The following quiz is based on MacNeil's approach. Answer each question **YES** or **NO**; then check your score below:

		YES	NO
1.	After greeting the caller, do you indicate your availability to help ("How may I help you?")?	☐	☐
2.	Once the caller has described the problem, do you *acknowledge* it and the customer's feelings ("I'm sorry you had a problem with our toaster.")?	☐	☐
3.	Do you ask questions to get as much information as you need to *assess the situation*?	☐	☐
4.	Do you listen closely and provide verbal clues to let the customer know you are listening attentively?	☐	☐
5.	Do you *affirm your understanding* of the problem by paraphrasing what the customer has told you?	☐	☐
6.	Do you give the customer the opportunity to clarify any points that may not have been clear to you?	☐	☐
7.	Next, do you *analyze the alternatives* to find a solution that is satisfying to both you and the customer?	☐	☐
8.	Finally, do you *agree on a plan* to resolve the problem?	☐	☐
9.	Do you thank the caller for contacting you?	☐	☐
10.	Do you follow through on any commitments or promises you've made to resolve the problem?	☐	☐

TOTAL NUMBER OF YES ANSWERS _____

DO YOU OFFER SOLUTIONS? If you answered all 10 questions **YES**, you are very conscientious in your approach to solving customer problems. Each step is an important part of the process, so any lower score is not acceptable.

UNFRIENDLY SOUNDING?
THAT DOES NOT COMPUTE!

Sounding friendly over the phone is an important first step to putting necessary interpersonal skills into practice. But, it's always a good idea to look for ways to improve. Answer each of the following questions **YES** or **NO** and then evaluate yourself below:

	YES	NO
1. Do you try to imagine the real human being with whom you're speaking?	☐	☐
2. Do you use empathetic words and phrases (such as "I understand") to show that you are paying close attention?	☐	☐
3. Do you try to smile when you answer the phone?	☐	☐
4. Do you give callers a friendly greeting?	☐	☐
5. Do you really try to be enthusiastic, even after a long day?	☐	☐
6. Do you use the customer's name during calls?	☐	☐
7. Do you speak clearly and naturally?	☐	☐
8. Do you treat all callers as though they are the best customers the company has?	☐	☐
9. Do you use "please," "thank you," and other words of courtesy and respect?	☐	☐
10. Do you give the caller your full attention — even if you've heard the same problem from several callers?	☐	☐
11. Do you avoid yawning or sounding tired on the phone?	☐	☐
12. Do you thank every caller?	☐	☐

TOTAL NUMBER OF YES ANSWERS _____

HOW 'REAL' DO YOU SOUND? Eleven or 12 **YES** answers suggests you convey warmth, friendliness, and professionalism over the phone. Nine or 10 is average. If you scored lower, try tape-recording some of your calls. Play back the recordings and determine whether you are conveying the warmth you'd like to. Then reread each question above and look for ways to implement each suggestion into everyday practice.

TAKE CALLERS' NAMES TO HEART

People take pride in their names. After all, our names define us as individuals. If you are unsure how to pronounce a caller's name, ask him or her. That would show that you care about getting his or her name right. Also, don't be afraid to apologize in advance if there's a chance you might say the name incorrectly. Callers appreciate when we treat their names with respect. To rate how effectively you use names, take the following quiz, answering **YES** or **NO** to each question; then check your score below:

		YES	NO
1.	Do you ask callers for their names and jot them down to refer to later in the conversation?	☐	☐
2.	When unsure, do you ask how the caller's name is spelled?	☐	☐
3.	Do you concentrate when callers state their names so they don't need to repeat them to you?	☐	☐
4.	Do you make a comment or funny remark when a name seems unusual to you?	☐	☐
5.	Do you clearly give your name when you answer the phone?	☐	☐
6.	If your name has an unusual spelling, do you automatically spell it out so the other person doesn't have to ask?	☐	☐
7.	Do you use the caller's name frequently in conversation?	☐	☐
8.	Do you refer to callers by their account numbers and avoid using their names?	☐	☐
9.	Do you double-check the spelling of your callers' names in your computer so you know the records are correct?	☐	☐
10.	When you like a caller's name, do you make a point of saying so ("That's a pretty first name")?	☐	☐

YOUR NAME RATING: The correct answer is **YES** to every question except Nos. 4 and 8. No. 4 is **NO** because no one likes to have his or her name ridiculed. And No. 8 is **NO** because referring to a person only by his or her account number is dehumanizing.

I KEEP SLIPPING INTO OLD PHONE HABITS

Do you ever wonder if your phone skills are losing polish and professionalism? One way to gauge your retention skills is to make a copy of this quiz. Mark your responses **YES** or **NO**, as they apply today. Take the quiz again in six months, and mark your responses in the second column. Then score yourself below:

	TODAY		IN SIX MONTHS	
	YES	NO	YES	NO
1. I answer within three rings.	☐	☐	☐	☐
2. I use a friendly salutation.	☐	☐	☐	☐
3. I ask callers how I can help.	☐	☐	☐	☐
4. If a call has to be transferred, I explain why.	☐	☐	☐	☐
5. I offer the name and number of the person to whom I'm transferring a call.	☐	☐	☐	☐
6. If I have to put a caller on hold, I ask his or her permission first.	☐	☐	☐	☐
7. I check back on holding callers every 30 seconds.	☐	☐	☐	☐
8. I thank each caller for holding.	☐	☐	☐	☐
9. I make callers feel confident that I know what I'm doing.	☐	☐	☐	☐
10. I always thank each caller for calling our company.	☐	☐	☐	☐
TOTALS	_____		_____	

YOUR SCORE: TODAY: If you responded **YES** to nine or 10 statements, you're doing an excellent job of handling the telephone. Eight is acceptable, but be sure to review the statements to which you responded **NO** and begin utilizing the tips suggested. **IN SIX MONTHS:** Only a score of 10 **YES** answers is acceptable.

KNOWING TELEPHONE TECHNIQUES PAYS OFF

Once telephone basics are second nature, you still should review them periodically. Those skills should serve each day as a structure upon which to build your abilities. The following quiz shows some additional ways to strengthen your relationship with callers. Read each statement and rate yourself from *1* to *5*, with *1* indicating you never practice that quality and *5* indicating that you always do:

	NEVER				ALWAYS
1. I return calls as quickly as possible.	*1*	*2*	*3*	*4*	*5*
2. I try to solve callers' problems as soon as I hear about them.	*1*	*2*	*3*	*4*	*5*
3. I am honest with callers.	*1*	*2*	*3*	*4*	*5*
4. I follow up with customers to confirm that a delivery was made on time.	*1*	*2*	*3*	*4*	*5*
5. I keep customers informed about our company's new products and services.	*1*	*2*	*3*	*4*	*5*
6. I direct customers to products and services that are the best value and choice for them.	*1*	*2*	*3*	*4*	*5*
7. I try to let customers know about special sale prices or quantity discounts.	*1*	*2*	*3*	*4*	*5*
8. I call customers we have not heard from lately.	*1*	*2*	*3*	*4*	*5*
9. I ask customers, "How is our company doing?"	*1*	*2*	*3*	*4*	*5*
10. I am prepared to answer any questions callers may have.	*1*	*2*	*3*	*4*	*5*

ARE YOU STILL IN TOUCH WITH PHONE BASICS? A score of 45–50 shows you are successfully using advanced phone skills to strengthen your relationship with customers on the telephone. A total of 39–44 points means you are doing a good job for customers but could do better. A score of 38 or less, however, indicates that you need to strengthen the advanced techniques that make customers happy. Read each statement on which you rated yourself **4** or less, and begin implementing the skills it describes in your phone work.

TIPS FROM THE FRONT LINE

The best telephone tips come from those who are there on the front line, fielding calls and responding to customer needs day in and day out. The readers of Dartnell's *Effective Telephone Techniques* newsletter continually provide an abundance of helpful telephone tips. The following quiz is based on some of these tips. See how well you are putting these ideas into practice. Respond **YES** or **NO** to each question; then score yourself below:

	YES	NO
1. If a caller corrects your pronunciation of his or her name, do you make an effort to say the name — correctly — in the conversation?	☐	☐
2. Do you pretend each call of the day is your first call, so that you are courteous and friendly all day long?	☐	☐
3. Do you try to emphasize what you can do, rather than what you can't do for callers? ("I can have that delivery there by noon tomorrow. Is that acceptable?")	☐	☐
4. After a difficult caller, do you take a brisk walk on your break so you are fresh and upbeat for the next customer?	☐	☐
5. To control the time you spend on the phone with chatty co-workers, do you suggest an alternative time to talk — like lunch or after work?	☐	☐
6. Do you jot down your voice-mail messages as you hear them, so you won't forget who needs to be called back?	☐	☐
7. Do you make some personalized conversation ("How's the weather there?") to show you're interested in the customer?	☐	☐

TOTAL NUMBER OF YES ANSWERS   _____

ARE YOU PHONE SAVVY? If you answered all seven questions **YES**, you've taken our readers' tips to heart. Five is average, but if you scored any lower, try putting some of these ideas into action.

Am I too chatty with callers?

Has a customer or co-worker ever complained that you are a little too chatty on the phone?

It can be very painful to hear criticism, especially when a customer is complaining about something you feel you're doing right. A little friendliness is good; you should not stop being friendly because of a customer's comments. However, this does present an opportunity for you to evaluate whether you've let your friendly nature get the best of you. The following quiz may help. Respond **Yes** or **No** to each statement; then check your score below:

	YES	NO
1. On more than one occasion, my boss has complained about how long I'm on the phone with customers.	☐	☐
2. Most of my customers know at least one detail about my private life.	☐	☐
3. I know the marital status of my customers — and they know mine.	☐	☐
4. I've been known to tell an occasional off-color joke or two to customers.	☐	☐
5. I've criticized co-workers to customers.	☐	☐
6. I share rumors that will interest customers.	☐	☐
7. I've tipped off customers about some changes within our company.	☐	☐
8. When customers place an order, I've sometimes inquired how they'll use the product.	☐	☐
9. When I'm having a bad day, I'll sometimes share my misery with a caller.	☐	☐
10. To keep from getting bored, I keep customers talking on the line for a few extra minutes.	☐	☐

TOTAL NUMBER OF YES ANSWERS _____

Are you too chatty? The only acceptable score is no **Yes** answers. If you responded **Yes** to even one statement, you probably have crossed the line with callers. Discuss with a co-worker (or your supervisor) just what parameters are acceptable for conversing with customers.

SHARPEN YOUR PHONE MANNERS

Telephone etiquette is everyone's business — from the "top dog" in your company on down to the production floor. Be sure you and your co-workers are well versed in the proper way to answer and use the phone.

Check out your knowledge of basic telephone courtesy with this quiz. Respond **YES** or **NO** to the following statements:

	YES	NO
1. I answer all "outside" calls with a friendly greeting, my name, and the name of my company or department.	☐	☐
2. I answer all "inside" calls with a friendly greeting and my name.	☐	☐
3. I answer the phone within three rings.	☐	☐
4. I talk distinctly into the telephone mouthpiece.	☐	☐
5. I ask callers how I can help them.	☐	☐
6. If a caller has to be transferred, I explain why.	☐	☐
7. I give callers the name and telephone number of the person to whom I'm transferring their call.	☐	☐
8. If I have to put a caller on hold, I ask for permission first.	☐	☐
9. When I put someone on hold, I use the hold feature on my phone. I don't just put down the receiver on my desk.	☐	☐
10. I check back with callers on hold every 30 seconds.	☐	☐
11. I thank each caller for holding.	☐	☐
12. I avoid slamming down the phone at the end of a call.	☐	☐
13. I give every caller my full attention. I don't try to do other work while talking on the phone.	☐	☐

TOTAL NUMBER OF YES ANSWERS _____

HOW'S YOUR TELEPHONE ETIQUETTE? If you responded **YES** to 12 or 13 of the above statements, you have great telephone manners. If you recorded 10 or 11 **YES** responses, you are probably courteous most of the time. If you scored nine or fewer **YES** responses, it's time to brush up on your phone skills.

PHONE REP, I LIKE YOUR ATTITUDE!

How do you send a positive impression to your customers during each call?

Boston-based customer service consultant Linda Ridgeway often leads her training sessions with the following quiz. Write the number that reflects the degree to which you **DISAGREE** or **AGREE** with each statement. Then check your score below:

DISAGREE				AGREE
1	2	3	4	5

1. The people I serve mean a lot to me. _____

2. I like treating customers the way I like to be treated when I call a business. _____

3. The public contact of customer service makes it enjoyable. _____

4. It's important to me that customers hang up feeling as though they've had a good experience with us. _____

5. Work and leisure often seem like one and the same to me. _____

6. On most days, I wake up energized about going to work. _____

7. I realize that callers can have a bad day, but I try to make it better with a positive attitude. _____

8. I put my personal problems on the back burner, so that they don't interfere with the attitude I convey to callers. _____

9. Even at the end of a frustrating day, I have a positive feeling about my job. _____

10. I'd feel as though something would be missing from my life if I pursued some other career path. _____

TOTAL SCORE _____

HOW DOES YOUR ATTITUDE RATE? A score of 41–50 is excellent. You obviously enjoy your work and send a very positive message to each caller. A score of 30–40 is average, but why be average? Try implementing the tips suggested in each statement. Says Ridgeway: "If you scored lower than 30, it's time for some serious reflection."

AM I FRIENDLY TO CALLERS?

The successful phone rep is one who always sounds professional but who also communicates interest and caring. Linda Winterburn, president of Success Exchange, a consulting firm in Mountain View, California, observes, "A friendly communicator knows how to approach others as a friend. Webster's *New World Dictionary* defines a friend as 'a person on the same side in a struggle … (an) ally, supporter, or sympathizer.'" Is that how you come across to those who call your business? Find out by taking the following quiz. Answer each question **YES** or **NO**; then check your score below:

	YES	NO
1. When customers call with a complaint, do you first let them know you are sorry they were inconvenienced?	☐	☐
2. Do you give upset callers all the time they need to vent their frustration?	☐	☐
3. Do you listen closely to what they are saying?	☐	☐
4. Do you show that you are listening by saying, "Yes," "uh-huh," or "I see"?	☐	☐
5. Do you avoid raising your voice to customers?	☐	☐
6. Do you try to convey that you are interested in helping every customer who calls?	☐	☐
7. In your conversations, do you include sincere friendly comments?	☐	☐
8. Do you convey enthusiasm?	☐	☐
9. When you're having a bad day, do you make every effort not to let it show to callers?	☐	☐
10. If you were on the other end of the line, would you honestly feel this phone rep (you) was friendly?	☐	☐

TOTAL NUMBER OF YES ANSWERS _____

DO YOU SOUND FRIENDLY TO CUSTOMERS? Eight to 10 **YES** answers gives you a high rating as a friendly phone rep. If you scored lower, review your **NO** responses and follow Linda Winterburn's guidance: "To promote friendly communication, incorporate the basic skills of answering questions, listening actively, and responding positively."

HOW WELL DO CALLERS RESPOND TO YOUR PHONE GREETING?

Most of us don't give our telephone greeting the attention it deserves, says Laurie Schloff, a senior consultant for The Speech Improvement Co. in Boston. Schloff emphasizes that *how* you deliver your phone greeting is as important as *what* you say. So, always speak clearly and not too quickly.

Because the phone greeting is so important, we're giving you this opportunity to test the quality of your phone greeting. Answer each question **YES** or **NO**. Then, check your score below:

		YES	NO
1.	Do you assume callers know who you are?	☐	☐
2.	Do you use a lengthy greeting?	☐	☐
3.	Do you often speak with co-workers while picking up the telephone?	☐	☐
4.	Do you identify yourself and say the name of your company?	☐	☐
5.	Do you clearly enunciate all the syllables in your name?	☐	☐
6.	Do you use a short, friendly greeting that conveys a professional tone?	☐	☐
7.	Do you speak too quickly to be understood?	☐	☐
8.	Do you put callers on hold without asking for their permission?	☐	☐
9.	Do you rush through the name of your company?	☐	☐
10.	Do you thank every caller for his or her call?	☐	☐

HOW'S YOUR PHONE GREETING? The correct responses to Question Nos. 1, 2, 3, 7, 8, and 9 are **NO**. You should have responded **YES** to Question Nos. 4, 5, 6, and 10. If you answered nine or more questions correctly, you take your telephone greeting seriously. Callers know what company they've reached, and they have a positive, professional impression of you and your organization.

If you answered eight or fewer questions correctly, you need to work on your phone greeting. It's worth the effort.

EVERYDAY PHONE CHALLENGES

How effective are your telephone skills in some of the most common situations reps encounter? Find out by asking yourself the following questions and checking the most appropriate response. (*Note:* More than one response may be acceptable.)

1. You must put a caller on hold. You:
   a. Make sure the caller has a nice radio station to listen to while he or she waits. ☐
   b. Put the caller on hold before he or she can object. ☐
   c. Ask first. ("Would you mind holding a moment?") ☐

2. You think you've dialed a wrong number. You:
   a. Ask, "What number is this?" ☐
   b. Apologize and check the number. ("Is this 555-2323?") ☐
   c. Make a joke such as: "I know I have the right number. Do you know what phone you've answered?" ☐

3. You need to call your doctor's office, but your office discourages using the phone for personal calls. You:
   a. Sneak in the call anyway. ☐
   b. Wait for your break, or call when you get home. ☐
   c. Ask the supervisor for this one exception. ☐

4. A caller becomes furious when you explain that you have to transfer his call. You:
   a. Say, "Life's rough," and transfer the call anyway. ☐
   b. Ignore the comment. ☐
   c. Say, "I'm sorry. I know how frustrating that can be." Then offer to have the appropriate person call the customer instead. ☐

HOW DO YOU HANDLE COMMON SITUATIONS? The correct answers are *1.* **(C)** (Don't make a caller hold without having a say in the matter.); *2.* **(B)** (The person you've reached, understandably, may be uncomfortable giving you a number [a], and humor is inappropriate to the situation [c].); *3.* **(B)** is best (but if that's impractical, ask a supervisor to make this rare exception [c].); *4.* **(C)** (Making a joke [a], or ignoring the comment [b], will only make the caller angrier.)

CUSTOMERS SEEK OTHER SIDE OF 'NO'

In situations where you can't meet callers' expectations, it's your job to make them just as happy with your solution as they would have been with their own. Take the following quiz to see if you are turning these potentially negative calls into positive experiences. Respond to each statement as **TRUE** or **FALSE**. Then check your score:

	TRUE	FALSE
1. It's important to hear every caller out before I make suggestions.	☐	☐
2. I illustrate the benefits of my solutions.	☐	☐
3. Sometimes, it's all right to flatly tell a caller "No."	☐	☐
4. I only make a promise to a caller if I can keep it.	☐	☐
5. If a difficult caller is relentless, I give in to the demands.	☐	☐
6. A good command of company policy, products, and services can help me keep control of calls.	☐	☐
7. If possible, I give callers a number of options so that the final decision is still theirs.	☐	☐
8. I focus on what I can give callers, not on what I can't.	☐	☐
9. Once a compromise is reached, I repeat the agreed-upon action to avoid confusion.	☐	☐
10. I accept that I can't please every caller — but I still try!	☐	☐

YOUR SCORE: In order to best serve customers, you should have answered **TRUE** to each statement except Nos. 3 and 5. It's important to remember to focus on the positive. Never just say "No," as No. 3 suggests. Instead, give a good reason, or, better yet, as No. 8 says, tell the caller what you can do. You set a dangerous precedent if you give in to unreasonable demands, as No. 5 states. It's not fair to your customers who do respect company policy.

STRENGTHEN YOUR PHONE VOICE

Fine-tune your voice for a good impression. The following quiz is based on ideas from Joan Kenley, a speech coach and author of *Voice Power* (Henry Holt). Answer each question **YES** or **NO**; then check your score below:

	YES	NO
1. Have you objectively evaluated your speaking voice on such qualities as whether you sound too breathy, flat, whispery, soft, or loud?	☐	☐
2. Have you asked a trusted friend or co-worker for a second opinion about your vocal quality?	☐	☐
3. Have you chosen one or two qualities you'd like to change about your voice?	☐	☐
4. Do you exhale evenly when you speak?	☐	☐
5. Have you begun morning "warm-up" exercises for your voice, such as singing loudly in the shower?	☐	☐
6. Do you avoid slouching while on the phone?	☐	☐
7. Have you tried standing up while talking on the phone?	☐	☐
8. Do you convey warmth and friendliness to callers by smiling while you're on the phone?	☐	☐
9. Have you begun paying closer attention to the voices of other reps — noting vocal qualities of theirs that you like?	☐	☐
10. In private, do you try adapting your voice to take on the qualities of other voices that you like?	☐	☐

TOTAL NUMBER OF YES ANSWERS _____

If you answered nine or more questions **YES**, you are making excellent progress in fine-tuning your speaking voice. Eight is average. If you answered seven or fewer questions **YES**, you need to devote more time and energy to improving how you sound to callers. Don't underestimate the value of your voice. It tells customers whether you are bored, tired, and uncaring — or happy, energetic, and enthusiastic.

WATCH YOUR LANGUAGE!

Keep in mind that words can nurture or nullify a good telephone dialogue. Do you speak well with customers when talking with them on the phone? Respond **YES** or **NO** to the following statements; then check your score below to determine if you are using proper telephone language:

IT IS PROPER TO: YES   NO

1. Use words that indicate that you understand the needs and requirements of the customer. ☐ ☐
2. Use industry "buzzwords" sparingly. ☐ ☐
3. Use brief and basic terminology. ☐ ☐
4. Tell the customer that you are a descendent of Daniel Webster and that you know every word in the dictionary. ☐ ☐
5. Use obscure, complicated scientific terms. ☐ ☐
6. Use words and phrases that your customer will have no problem understanding. ☐ ☐
7. Speak in the present tense to add action and feeling to your conversation. ☐ ☐
8. Use the same words often. ☐ ☐
9. Indicate your importance by saying "I" and "me" often. ☐ ☐
10. Use words and phrases that help the customer visualize what you are saying. ☐ ☐

HOW'S YOUR TELEPHONE LANGUAGE? Statement Nos. 4, 5, 8, and 9 are not proper ways to use language when talking with customers on the telephone. Here's why: **STATEMENT NO. 4:** The phrase is an instant turnoff. Let your use of appropriate language show the customer that you know what you're talking about. **STATEMENT NO. 5:** If you use obscure words and phrases, you'll look foolish and convey to the customer that you aren't in touch with his or her needs. **STATEMENT NO. 8:** Repeating the same words may make you sound like a broken record. Demonstrate verbal variety to communicate on an appropriate level with the customer. **STATEMENT NO. 9:** It is better to use words like "we" and "us" to indicate that you are part of an entire team that's interested in meeting your customer's needs.
KEY POINT: Develop language skills to show professionalism, not to impress.

CHAPTER 6
SELLING SKILLS
STEP OUT AHEAD OF THE COMPETITION

In today's competitive environment, selling is more than simply delivering a product or service. Selling also involves offering value and quality, providing satisfaction, building trust, handling objections, and developing new strategies for new offerings. For sales personnel, having excellent communication and presentation skills are no longer just an option; they're a necessity.

The quizzes in this section will help you and your sales employees evaluate their sales skills and troubleshoot problem areas that may be limiting their potential. The commentary accompanying each quiz provides suggestions that help your salespeople hone their talents and develop that sharper edge that makes the difference between a good sales force and a great sales force.

Are your salespeople going above and beyond customer expectations? The best salespeople, those who know their customers, are better able to establish rapport and build long-term relationships with them. How well informed is your sales force? Have your salespeople take the quiz on "How to Build Prospect Empathy" to evaluate how well they understand the needs of their potential customers, how aware their customers are of your company's products and services, and how capable they are at building relationships with their customers.

Do you suspect that some members of your sales force might not be keeping up with ongoing changes in the market? Do you want to remind your salespeople that today's customers are increasingly better educated and informed and that they expect a clear, precise, and technologically astute selling approach? Have them take the quiz "Professional Selling Is Changing" to rate their sales techniques.

Are your salespeople striving for personal and professional excellence by creating new business? Servicing current customers well is critically important to your continued success, but building your customer base is also a way to add to your bottom line. Use the quiz "Do You Fear Making Cold Calls?" to encourage your salespeople to contact new prospects, discover innovative applications for your products, and overcome their apprehension of this difficult but effective activity.

When a member of your sales force makes a sale, everybody in the company benefits. When what you sell enables customers to achieve their objectives and improve their competitive edge, you keep those customers coming back. That's how your company measures success. The quizzes in this section will allow you to track and enhance the sales performance that will help you maintain that success.

ARE YOU AN EFFECTIVE SALESPERSON?

Are you constantly striving to improve your sales skills and techniques? Answer **YES** or **NO** in response to the following statements to determine if they are effective selling techniques to use:

	YES	NO
1. My follow-up correspondence is accurate, precise, and brief.	☐	☐
2. I don't make sales calls on Fridays because my customers are only thinking about the weekend.	☐	☐
3. I recognize that written communication supports my selling efforts.	☐	☐
4. I continually prospect to maintain a list of potential customers.	☐	☐
5. I fill in unforeseen changes in my schedule with cold calls.	☐	☐
6. I mail my company's brochure to 10 new prospects each week.	☐	☐
7. I memorize my product literature.	☐	☐
8. I know the strengths and weaknesses of my competition.	☐	☐
9. I use the latest technological tools available to support my account and market coverage.	☐	☐

SCORING: Statement Nos. 2, 6, and 7 are not highly effective sales methods. Here's why:

STATEMENT NO. 2: Many customers have a lighter schedule on Fridays and may have more time to spend with you. In addition, if other salespeople take Friday off, it leaves all the customers for you.

STATEMENT NO. 6: This is not an effective way of advertising your company unless you know your primary contact and understand why the customer needs your product or service. It is more effective to qualify a potential account before sending information.

STATEMENT NO. 7: Memorizing your product literature can consume valuable time. Become familiar with the information, but only memorize when you need it for fast retrieval.

KEY POINT: Establish proficient methods that work for you to achieve a balance of work and leisure and to make your selling career a success.

PROFESSIONAL SELLING IS CHANGING

Professional selling is changing due to a more global competitive marketplace. Are you keeping up with the ongoing changes? What are the most critical differences? Answer **YES** or **NO** to indicate whether the following statements are true of the selling profession today:

SALESPEOPLE TODAY:	YES	NO
1. are relationship builders and solution providers.	☐	☐
2. use hard-driving closing methods.	☐	☐
3. use a more consultative selling approach.	☐	☐
4. feel a confrontational selling style works the best.	☐	☐
5. think the sale ends with the close.	☐	☐
6. are using closing techniques that allow them to listen and respond to the customer.	☐	☐
7. want to create a feeling of comfort for the customer.	☐	☐
8. know less than their customers.	☐	☐
9. need to treat customers with respect and dignity.	☐	☐
10. realize customers still want a slick presentation.	☐	☐

SCORING: Statement Nos. 2, 4, 5, and 10 are not selling methods that work well with today's customers. Here's why:

STATEMENT NO. 2: Professional salespeople today do not use hard-driving closing methods. Customers are turned off by a strong-arm approach and will not tolerate being bullied.

STATEMENT NO. 4: Overbearing, demanding salespeople are ineffective and a thing of the past. Customers are more knowledgeable today: They will avoid confrontation and refuse to buy.

STATEMENT NO. 5: Closing is no longer the final step to a sale. When the customer decides to buy, the professional salesperson's work has just begun. Repeat business and long-term relationships are more important than just obtaining a purchase.

STATEMENT NO. 10: Today's customers are turned off by a slick presentation. They marvel at new technology, but if a presentation is not clear and precise, they will refuse to buy.

KEY POINT: Upgrade your selling skills and jump into the new sales arena for tremendous sales success.

GENERATING SALES LEADS: ARE YOU GETTING YOUR SHARE?

Generating sales leads should be one of your top priorities. Are you aware of all the ways you can generate sales leads? Take the following quiz and find out! Indicate whether you use each of the following sales-generating techniques:

		YES	NO
1.	Referrals from satisfied customers	☐	☐
2.	Personal letters	☐	☐
3.	Networking	☐	☐
4.	Cold calling	☐	☐
5.	Telemarketing	☐	☐
6.	Attending local events	☐	☐
7.	Advertising	☐	☐
8.	Offering to speak at local events	☐	☐
9.	Direct mail	☐	☐
10.	Taking excellent care of current customers	☐	☐
11.	Joining or forming a "leads" group	☐	☐
12.	Acting as a sponsor or committee member for a local event	☐	☐
13.	Testimonials	☐	☐
14.	Joining clubs or organizations	☐	☐
15.	Contacts from mutual acquaintances	☐	☐
16.	Social gatherings or events	☐	☐

TOTAL NUMBER OF YES ANSWERS _____

WHAT'S YOUR SCORE? If you're using at least a dozen of these methods to generate leads, congratulations! We'll bet you have no trouble finding enough people to call on. Those of you who are relying heavily on just a few of these methods may be experiencing difficulty generating the leads you need for continued success. Most successful salespeople use as many avenues as they can think of for generating leads. This not only adds interest to the selling job but enables you to find people you would otherwise not be aware of and not be able to find.

DO YOU FEAR MAKING COLD CALLS?

The more cold calls you make, the more doors of opportunity open for you to make your selling career a success.

Respond with a **YES** to those statements below that represent effective approaches to cold calls and **NO** to those that don't:

	YES	NO
1. I feel confident when I make an introductory call to a new prospect.	☐	☐
2. I prefer to make calls on repeat customers rather than strangers.	☐	☐
3. I don't think cold calls generate sales and profits.	☐	☐
4. I don't take rejection from new prospects personally.	☐	☐
5. I fill in canceled meetings with cold calls.	☐	☐
6. I have trouble getting past a receptionist when making cold calls.	☐	☐
7. I make my presentation to the first person who will see me at a new account.	☐	☐
8. I have various methods of approaching new accounts who initially make it hard to call on them.	☐	☐
9. I work hard to make a good first impression.	☐	☐
10. I have effective goals and objectives with respect to making cold calls.	☐	☐

SCORING: Statement Nos. 2, 3, 6, and 7 are not effective methods of thinking about cold calls. Here's why:

STATEMENT NO. 2: Remember that regular customers were called on the first time by somebody. Consider prospects as future regular accounts.

STATEMENT NO. 3: It's more expensive to find new accounts than to maintain regular customers. However, your future lies with new business and new applications for your products or services.

STATEMENT NO. 6: This can be a difficult task. Make the frontline person realize you have information that will improve his or her position or situation, and this "gatekeeper" will let you pass.

STATEMENT NO. 7: Determine the best candidate to hear your story.

HOW TO BUILD PROSPECT EMPATHY

Empathy means understanding the obligations and motivating circumstances that influence each prospect. How do you improve your ability to empathize with your prospect before your first meeting? Answer **YES** or **NO** in response to the following questions to determine if they help you empathize with your prospects:

	YES	NO
1. What do you already know about the prospect?	☐	☐
2. Does the prospect know anything about you or your company?	☐	☐
3. Does the prospect respond to powerful closing techniques?	☐	☐
4. Is the prospect aware of your products and services?	☐	☐
5. What does the prospect require from your company?	☐	☐
6. Can you fulfill the prospect's current needs?	☐	☐
7. How quickly can you sell the prospect?	☐	☐
8. Does the prospect constantly have problems?	☐	☐
9. What is the prospect's reputation in the marketplace?	☐	☐

SCORING: Be careful with information gathered from Question Nos. 3, 7, and 8. The answers can draw you to the wrong conclusions. Here's why:

QUESTION NO. 3: This information won't help you unless the prospect has a definite interest in your product or service.

QUESTION NO. 7: This information is difficult to predetermine. Certain products or services require long sales cycles, and you may not be able to sell the prospect quickly.

QUESTION NO. 8: Are you asking this question as a problem solver or a problem avoider? A prospect who has a variety of problems may be a high potential candidate for your products and services.

Empathy requires truly wanting to understand your prospect's needs and requirements. Empathize with prospects, and you will establish lasting relationships that will prolong your selling career.

Establishing Total Trust

Your anxiety from attempting to make the prospect buy from you will decrease as your level of trust increases. Customers who completely trust the salespeople who call on them will normally buy as much as possible from them.

Answer **Yes** or **No** in response to the following statements to determine if they are trust-building methods:

		Yes	No
1.	Make the prospect understand your point of view.	☐	☐
2.	Keep all your promises and commitments.	☐	☐
3.	Maintain a high level of honesty and integrity.	☐	☐
4.	Show professional courtesy to every person at the prospect's business.	☐	☐
5.	Pursue the prospect because of your desire to win the account.	☐	☐
6.	Make sure the prospect knows what you expect from a long-term relationship.	☐	☐
7.	Be loyal to the prospect and trash his or her competitors.	☐	☐
8.	Offer apologies when you make a mistake.	☐	☐
9.	Ask the prospect for feedback on your performance.	☐	☐
10.	Give the prospect "I" messages, such as "I agree with your purchasing methods."	☐	☐

Scoring: Statement Nos. 1, 5, 6, 7, and 9 are not proper statements to build complete trust with a prospect. Here's why:

Statement No. 1: Make sure you understand the prospect's point of view before you present your own opinions.

Statement No. 5: Pursue the sale and work toward a situation where you and the prospect both gain something of value from the relationship.

Statement No. 6: Develop a list of mutual expectations where both you and the prospect know what to anticipate from each other.

Statement No. 7: Be loyal to anyone who is not present during your discussions. Trashing the competition won't raise your status with your customer.

Statement No. 9: Provide feedback to the prospect on his or her company's performance, too.

GETTING PROSPECTS TO 'OPEN UP'

Using a questioning process that encourages your customers to "open up" and offer enough information is crucial to success. If you're not careful, though, you can ask questions that make the customer uncomfortable and unwilling to divulge important information.

Do you ask pertinent and proper questions, or do you ask inappropriate, "nosy" ones?

Answer **YES** or **NO** in response to the following questions to indicate whether they're proper or improper inquiries:

		YES	NO
1.	"If I demonstrate that my equipment will save you 30 percent in operation costs, will you buy it?"	☐	☐
2.	"Have you been passed over for promotion and gotten stuck in the job of purchasing?"	☐	☐
3.	"How many new products will you offer to your marketplace next year?"	☐	☐
4.	"Have I delivered on all my promises to you?"	☐	☐
5.	"Do you realize my competition believes you give false information about your product costs?"	☐	☐
6.	"Will you give me a larger share of your business if I can improve your efficiency?"	☐	☐
7.	"Will you accept a price increase if I change from once-a-week to twice-a-week delivery?"	☐	☐
8.	"What are your political views?"	☐	☐

SCORING: Question Nos. 2, 5, and 8 are improper inquiries. Here's why:

QUESTION NO. 2: Are you assuming that the purchasing agent is incompetent? Never belittle this position.

QUESTION NO. 5: Are you trying to downgrade the competition or accuse the buyer of giving false information? This question could alienate your contact and prevent you from establishing a business relationship.

QUESTION NO. 8: Stay away from politics and religion. You could lose the sale because of differences that have nothing to do with the features and benefits of your merchandise.

ARE YOU HANDLING YOUR FOLLOW-UP WITH FLAIR?

Follow-up is one of the most important parts of the sales process. That's because most sales can only be consummated after a considerable amount of follow-up.

But follow-up should always be planned well in advance and carefully executed according to that plan.

The following quiz will help you to gauge your follow-up approach.

		YES	NO
1.	Do you routinely plan a follow-up agenda?	☐	☐
2.	Do you approach your prospects a little differently each time you follow up?	☐	☐
3.	Do you know which prospects are or are not worthy of your follow-up?	☐	☐
4.	Do you record the details associated with each specific follow-up effort?	☐	☐
5.	Do you allow adequate time between each follow-up effort?	☐	☐
6.	Do you avoid waiting before you follow up?	☐	☐
7.	Do you consider the needs of your prospects when you plan your follow-up efforts?	☐	☐
8.	Do you consider, in advance, how much time you will need for each follow-up effort?	☐	☐
9.	Do you plan to make specific progress with each follow-up effort?	☐	☐
10.	Do you try new tactics for each follow-up effort?	☐	☐
11.	Do you make an effort to learn more about your prospects with each follow-up effort?	☐	☐
12.	Do you press for a close with each follow-up effort?	☐	☐

SCORING: The correct response in each case is **YES**. Excellent: Ten or more correct answers indicate that you are very effective at follow-up. Good: Eight or nine correct answers indicate that your follow-up techniques are good and need only minor improvement. Fair: Fewer than eight correct answers suggest that your follow-up approach needs to be reconsidered. *Remember:* Successful selling always requires proper follow-up!

WHAT IS AN OBJECTION — REALLY?

How do you define an objection? Do you consider objections opportunities to learn more about your customers' needs? Answer **Yes** or **No** in response to the following statements to determine if they are a proper way to think about objections:

	Yes	No
1. An objection is not always an obstacle to closing the sale.	☐	☐
2. An objection that is mishandled can be a barrier to completing the sale.	☐	☐
3. An objection can lead to a sale.	☐	☐
4. Objections are not a normal part of selling.	☐	☐
5. You should not plan on encountering objections.	☐	☐
6. Objections should be discussed thoroughly.	☐	☐
7. Most objections are questions in disguise.	☐	☐
8. An objection means the customer is not going to buy.	☐	☐
9. One of the best ways to overcome objections is to read Dartnell's *Overcoming Objections* newsletter.	☐	☐
10. Your attitude should be, "I will overcome every objection with which I am confronted."	☐	☐

Scoring: Statement Nos. 4, 5, 8, and 10 are not proper ways to consider objections. Here's why:

Statement No. 4: Objections are a common occurrence. They are a mechanism through which the customer can make sure he or she is making a good buying decision.

Statement No. 5: It may seem like a negative approach, but your product or service is probably not perfect, and you should prepare for objections from the customer.

Statement No. 8: An objection may be the last obstacle before the customer buys. When the customer puts up a red flag, your order may be just around the corner if you resolve the issue.

Statement No. 10: This statement may lead to disappointment. You should certainly do everything you can to resolve objections, but don't continue to waste time with an impossible issue that will not add value to you or the customer.

HANDLING OBJECTIONS LIKE A PRO

How do professional salespeople handle objections? What are some effective methods of managing and overcoming obstacles? Answer **YES** or **NO** in response to the following statements to determine if they are productive methods of handling objections:

	YES	NO
1. If you can immediately overcome an objection, confirm that your customer agrees with your resolution.	☐	☐
2. Listen carefully to the explanation of the problem given by the customer.	☐	☐
3. Explain that you have a support staff who responds to all customer problems.	☐	☐
4. Tell the customer you have never heard that particular objection before, and suggest he or she do more research.	☐	☐
5. Rephrase the concern back to the customer to make sure you have a good understanding of the issue.	☐	☐
6. Lower the price immediately because you know that will solve all problems.	☐	☐
7. Once you have thoroughly explored an objection, continue with your presentation to give the customer more information.	☐	☐
8. Use a precise questioning process to get the customer to explain the problem in detail.	☐	☐
9. If you do know the complete solution to the objection, carefully answer all questions and solve the problem.	☐	☐

SCORING: Statement Nos. 3, 4, and 6 are not good objection-handling techniques. Here's why:

STATEMENT NO. 3: Don't avoid objections. If you refer all your problems to someone else, you will lose credibility.

STATEMENT NO. 4: This is just another way of evading the issue.

STATEMENT NO. 6: This just opens up another can of worms. You may eventually resolve the issue, but end up with lower sales and profits because of your too-quick response.

MAKING FULL USE OF SELLING TIME

Having a clear daily plan on how you'll use your time can make a difference between being a mediocre salesperson and becoming a high-powered sales pro.

Do you make a concerted effort to use your time effectively during working hours? To find out, take the following quiz, based on Jim Schneider's book, *The Feel of Success in Selling* (Prentice Hall):

		YES	NO
1.	Do you sell only by appointment — so that sales time is quality time?	☐	☐
2.	Do you carry a pocket-size list of your 20 best prospects at all times — so that you can use a few minutes of unexpected free time to strengthen your relationship with them?	☐	☐
3.	Do you write a "to-do" list each night for the next day?	☐	☐
4.	Do you take a few moments at the beginning of each day to envision the day ahead?	☐	☐
5.	Do you make your sales calls in concentrated, well-planned bursts of selling, rather than spreading them out throughout your schedule?	☐	☐
6.	Do you build a network of referral sources who will sell for you?	☐	☐
7.	Do you avoid overscheduling in order to spend quality time with your prospects?	☐	☐
8.	Do you ruthlessly qualify your prospects before investing too much time with them?	☐	☐
9.	Do you respond immediately to customer inquiries?	☐	☐
10.	When your list of prospects becomes short, do you set aside time to prospect by phone or mail?	☐	☐
11.	Do you continually refer to your goals throughout the day and ask yourself, "What's the best use of my sales time right now?"	☐	☐

SCORING: The correct answer to each question is YES.

Successful sales pros look for better ways to work with what is immediately at hand. The pros know that sales time is as precious as gold, and they stay focused on what they need to accomplish.

ARE YOU WELL-ORGANIZED?

Do others in your company admire you for your organizational abilities? Are your call reports up-to-date and finished on time? Do your customers appreciate your accurate and timely follow-up and follow-through? Respond **YES** or **NO** to the following statements to indicate if they reflect a professional approach to organization:

	YES	NO
1. I can retrieve a call report concerning any customer within minutes.	☐	☐
2. I know my top 10 primary tasks when I start work in the morning.	☐	☐
3. I accomplish most of my daily goals.	☐	☐
4. I clear my desk of all reading material once a week.	☐	☐
5. Occasionally I get letters that begin, "You haven't gotten back to me yet, so...?"	☐	☐
6. I rarely take work home.	☐	☐
7. I allow for frequent interruptions — whether they are phone calls or visitors — when I'm in my office.	☐	☐
8. I work better when an issue becomes an emergency or panic situation.	☐	☐
9. My call reports are written succinctly and get right to the point.	☐	☐
10. I avoid being preoccupied with details, so I can stay active pursuing new opportunities.	☐	☐

SCORING: Statement Nos. 2, 3, 5, and 8 are not good examples of effective organizational ability. Here's why:

STATEMENT NO. 2: This is an example of a fair organizational method. You will develop better skills if you limit your primary daily tasks to two or three.

STATEMENT NO. 3: This is a vague statement. If you fail to complete any necessary task, you should move it to the top of the next day's list.

STATEMENT NO. 5: You are in trouble if you receive a letter like this from a customer. Prompt follow-up is a sign of a highly organized salesperson.

STATEMENT NO. 8: You may work well during a crisis, but often you will scare away customers who want calmer and more organized salespeople working with them.

HOW'S YOUR MENTAL ATTITUDE?

Do you have a positive mental attitude and a commitment to serve your company and customers? A combination of excellent selling skills and a high level of motivation can produce tremendous results. Analyze your attitude and answer **YES** or **NO** in response to the following statements to determine if you have a positive approach to your profession:

	YES	NO
1. I wear expensive clothes to look good for my customers.	☐	☐
2. I preach my high level of enthusiasm so my customers realize my commitment to them.	☐	☐
3. I am enthusiastic and self-motivated, and have a positive mental attitude.	☐	☐
4. I follow through on all promises to emphasize my dependability.	☐	☐
5. I am confident and not easily discouraged.	☐	☐
6. I only call on enthusiastic, dynamic customers.	☐	☐
7. I practice my presentations to keep them focused.	☐	☐
8. I believe being happy and optimistic will always win the customer.	☐	☐
9. I welcome constructive criticism because I want to improve and refine my selling skills.	☐	☐
10. I am creative and make effective decisions when solving problems and overcoming objections.	☐	☐

SCORING: Statement Nos. 1, 2, 6, and 8 are not good examples of maintaining a positive mental attitude. Here's why:

STATEMENT NO. 1: Your appearance should be neat and orderly. Trying to overly impress your customers will make them consider you flashy and self-centered. You will appear more concerned about yourself than them.

STATEMENT NO. 2: Demonstrate your enthusiasm, but don't preach it.

STATEMENT NO. 6: Don't judge your customers by their initial level of enthusiasm. They could be steadfast, dedicated participants in a diverse market.

STATEMENT NO. 8: A positive attitude will definitely help close the sale. However, customer knowledge and awareness of needs and requirements are equally important.

SETTING *POSITIVE* GOALS!

Do you set positive — yet attainable — goals that help you work hard for your future? Do you reinforce your goals with positive affirmations? Find out by responding **YES** if you think the statement is a positive way to state your goals or **NO** if you think it isn't:

	YES	NO
1. I keep my goal statements personal: "I enjoy my work and I will earn more money this year."	☐	☐
2. I challenge myself: "I know it won't be easy, but I will close all my accounts this month."	☐	☐
3. I use action modifiers when describing my goals: "I will regularly finish all my follow-up."	☐	☐
4. I'm realistic about my goals: "I probably won't accomplish it, but I intend to earn $100,000 this year."	☐	☐
5. I use words that convey emotion: "I will enthusiastically make one cold call per day!"	☐	☐
6. I keep my goal statements short and concise: "I'll write my call reports at the end of each sales call."	☐	☐
7. I establish far-reaching goals: "I will become a sales manager within the next 20 years."	☐	☐
8. I use terms that imply I have already accomplished my goals: "I will completely learn the basic characteristics of the five top-selling products that we sell by the end of the month."	☐	☐
9. I avoid making goals that compare me to others: "I will perform my job to the best of my ability."	☐	☐

SCORING: Statement Nos. 2, 4, and 7 are not affirmative comments. Here's why:

STATEMENT NO. 2: It's good to challenge yourself, but don't put a defeating clause in your statement. Simply say: "I will close a majority of my accounts."

STATEMENT NO. 4: If you don't feel $100,000 is attainable, state a figure that is.

STATEMENT NO. 7: You might as well make it "40 years." Why can't you be a sales manager next year?

RIDING THE 'SALES ROLLER COASTER'

All salespeople have their ups and downs — sales cycles that have peaks and valleys. Closing cycles can follow the same pattern. You can have a day in which many prospects say "Yes, I'll buy," followed by a day in which almost everyone says "No, I won't buy."

How do you keep yourself moving forward in a positive direction?

Respond **YES** to these statements if they indicate ways to keep you "on track," and **NO** if they don't:

	YES	NO
1. When customers begin to say "No," I think back to my most recent successful selling experience.	☐	☐
2. I consider everything that's gone wrong during a sales call that had a negative result.	☐	☐
3. I mentally "pump myself up" before a presentation.	☐	☐
4. I associate with other unsuccessful closers to learn which techniques don't work.	☐	☐
5. I seek out people who will provide positive support.	☐	☐
6. I always take a new product or service to a current friendly account to practice my presentation.	☐	☐
7. I always worry about not being able to close a sale.	☐	☐
8. I accept rejection as a defeat and work hard to avoid it.	☐	☐
9. I learn more from my sales failures than from my sales successes.	☐	☐

SCORING: Statement Nos. 2, 4, 7, and 8 are events that will make your sales career seem like a roller coaster ride.

Here's why:

STATEMENT NO. 2: Be aware of circumstances that prevented a sale, but don't dwell on them. Stress the positive events.

STATEMENT NO. 4: Misery loves company. Search out successful closers and learn their techniques.

STATEMENT NO. 7: Don't fret. Always expect to close the sale. Your customer may refuse to buy only because you appear worried or concerned.

STATEMENT NO. 8: Rejection is not a defeat. It is merely an obstacle to making a buying decision.

ARE CLOSING QUESTIONS TOUGH FOR YOU TO ASK?

Do you feel some degree of discomfort asking closing questions?

If you do, you're not alone. This discomfort can be the result of past difficulties with asking closing questions — mainly because of the awkwardness involved.

Take the following quiz to see just how comfortable you are in asking closing questions:

	YES	NO
1. I usually don't prepare my closing questions before trying to close.	☐	☐
2. I usually use the same type of closing questions with each customer.	☐	☐
3. I usually feel a great deal of anxiety prior to asking a closing question.	☐	☐
4. Some customers have told me that I don't try to close as often as I should.	☐	☐
5. I've often been told by customers that I come across as being "pushy" when I try to close.	☐	☐
6. Following a sales call, I am often angry at myself for not asking a closing question, even though I know I should have.	☐	☐
7. I don't like to ask closing questions because I don't want to put pressure on my customers.	☐	☐
8. I often ask for help from associates in closing significant customers.	☐	☐
9. Closing questions are a problem for me because I usually don't know the best time to pose them.	☐	☐
10. It's difficult to ask a closing question — even when I'm convinced that the customer is ready to buy.	☐	☐

SCORING: If you responded to more than five statements with **YES**, you probably have trouble asking closing questions.

OBSERVE BODY LANGUAGE: IT'S A KEY CLOSING CLUE

Confused as to whether your prospect is ready to buy? There are several nonverbal indicators you can look for, besides the more obvious vocal ones.

Body language can say a lot. Be ready to interpret it, and you'll be quicker to see the signs of a customer ready to buy. Take this quiz:

	YES	NO
1. Does the prospect lean forward to peruse your final contract?	☐	☐
2. Do you receive a hearty handshake in your face-to-face meetings with this prospect?	☐	☐
3. Does the prospect give you his or her undivided attention and good eye contact during your communications?	☐	☐
4. Is your prospect relaxed and happy to see you?	☐	☐
5. Does your prospect jot down notes during your presentation?	☐	☐
6. Does your prospect nod in agreement over the statements you make?	☐	☐
7. Does your prospect carefully study your handouts?	☐	☐
8. Does your prospect face and lean forward slightly toward you when you're talking?	☐	☐
9. Do your prospect's facial expressions indicate happiness rather than confusion and displeasure?	☐	☐
10. Does your prospect refrain from fidgeting, pencil tapping, and other restless habits that indicate boredom?	☐	☐

TOTAL NUMBER OF YES ANSWERS _____

SCORING: Answering **YES** to one or more of the above questions regarding each prospect is good news for you — because the prospect is giving you favorable indications via his or her body language.

The more questions you answer **YES** to in regard to each of your prospects, the riper this person is as a potential buyer.

So be as attentive to what each of your prospects does as you are to what each of them says.

REALLY THANKING YOUR CUSTOMERS

Customers warrant continual acknowledgment for giving salespeople their business. Saying "Thank you" is appropriate, but customers today need more. Answer **YES** or **NO** in response to the following statements to indicate whether they are appropriate ways of expressing appreciation:

	YES	NO
1. Call the customer frequently to evaluate the performance of your product or service.	☐	☐
2. Ask the people who actually use your product or service if they are receiving all the expected value.	☐	☐
3. Give the customer a list of people to call if any problems occur.	☐	☐
4. Once your customer is using your product or service, raise the price to demonstrate the real value.	☐	☐
5. Have periodic meetings with all the users of your product or service to help them learn how to use it more efficiently.	☐	☐
6. Send information on a regular basis that describes other uses of your product or service.	☐	☐
7. Send a letter to all the customer's competitors on how well the product or service is working, and copy your customer.	☐	☐
8. Send thank-you notes after every sales call to continue to demonstrate your appreciation.	☐	☐
9. An invitation for an occasional lunch or dinner will show your appreciation and provide you with time to discuss additional products and services.	☐	☐

SCORING: Statement Nos. 3, 4, and 7 are not proper methods of expressing your appreciation for your customers' business. Here's why:

STATEMENT NO. 3: Your customer will want to talk with you first if a problem occurs. Show your appreciation by being available to work out difficulties personally.

STATEMENT NO. 4: A price increase does not say "Thank you." Don't immediately raise a price unless agreed to previously.

STATEMENT NO. 7: This procedure may be more for your benefit than the customer's. Ask for permission from your buyer before you begin to use his or her use of your product or service as a testimonial.

DO YOU SATISFY YOUR CUSTOMERS?

Are you meeting all of your customers' expectations? Do you know all of their needs and requirements? Is customer gratification one of your primary goals? Answer **YES** or **NO** in response to the following statements to find out whether or not you are completely satisfying your customers:

		YES	NO
1.	I treat my customers with respect and courtesy.	☐	☐
2.	I laugh at and ridicule other salespeople when I am in the role of a customer.	☐	☐
3.	I have thorough knowledge of my products and services.	☐	☐
4.	I have thorough knowledge of my customers' products, companies, and industries.	☐	☐
5.	I wait for problems to occur with my competitors at my customer accounts so I can get a higher price for my products and services.	☐	☐
6.	I have thorough knowledge of my customers' strengths and weaknesses.	☐	☐
7.	I read newsletters and trade publications from my customers' industries.	☐	☐
8.	I understand my customers' target industries and can make suggestions to help them strengthen their presence in these markets.	☐	☐
9.	I review my customers' applications of my products to maintain an end user's point of view.	☐	☐

SCORING: Statement Nos. 1, 2, and 5 are not effective ways of evaluating your performance in meeting your customers' requirements. Here's why:

STATEMENT NO. 1: This is a good rule. However, expand it to include everyone you meet, because he or she may be your next customer.

STATEMENT NO. 2: Don't laugh or ridicule. Instead, observe and learn from the salesperson's strengths and weaknesses.

STATEMENT NO. 5: You may be too late if you wait for a problem to occur. Trying to raise costs when you solve a problem will definitely not help you with future orders.

CHAPTER 7
SELF-DEVELOPMENT
PERSONAL CHARACTERISTICS CAN MAKE OR BREAK A CAREER

We've all known people who were talented and well trained for their jobs, yet miserable themselves and difficult for others to work with. Both job satisfaction and successful integration into a work group ultimately depend as much on personality factors as they do on task-performance skills.

Adapting a unique personality to a job begins with introspection: honestly assessing individual strengths, weaknesses, preferences and quirks. Invite your employees to get to know themselves better with such quizzes as "Are You Logical or Intuitive?" and "What Drives Your Competitiveness?"

Though no one lists social graces on a résumé, how employees present themselves to others makes an enormous difference in their ability to win the trust of customers and the cooperation of colleagues. Use "Are You

Minding Your Manners?" and "Cultivate Your Charisma" to focus attention on social skills.

Why is it that given the exact same job description and working condi-
tions, one person loves coming to work while another starts watching the
clock the moment he or she arrives? In this section you'll find quizzes
that assess a number of factors affecting morale, such as depression ("Do
You Feel Disenchanted?"), burnout ("Making Time for Yourself") and
boredom ("Make Work More Interesting").

Does the job allow the employee to do what he or she does and loves
doing best? Explore job/talent match with "What's Your Personal Long
Suit?" Does the employee see the job leading to personal long term goals
and aspirations? Encourage personal articulation of such goals with
"What's Your Lifetime Plan?".

As important as personal characteristics and feelings are to working
relationships, many work groups have difficulty communicating frankly
with each other about such matters. Any of the quizzes in this section can
serve as a departure point for group discussion. They can be used to
broach a sensitive subject or as a warm-up to facilitate personal sharing at
a staff meeting. For best results, ask each member of the group to complete the quiz individually and suggest that they disclose as little or as
much as they feel comfortable sharing with the group. These quizzes can
be a fun and eye-opening way for employees to assess self-knowledge and
their ability to work together productivity and happily with others.

ARE YOU LOGICAL OR INTUITIVE?

When communicating with your co-workers, it helps to know what makes you choose to act or think in a certain way. People's actions are dominated either by the right or left side of the brain. Someone with left-brain dominance responds to the literal meaning of words. This person's strength is logic. A person with right-brain dominance tends to focus more on tone of voice and body language than on actual words. This person's strength is intuition. Find out what side of the brain influences your life by circling the appropriate letter:

1. My work space is:
   a. Neat and orderly.
   b. Disorganized and somewhat chaotic.

2. I prefer:
   a. To end one task before starting another.
   b. Juggling different tasks at the same time.

3. When something good or bad happens to me, I:
   a. Talk about it immediately.
   b. Talk about it only after some reflection.

4. When I go to restaurants, I like to:
   a. Stay with the standard menu.
   b. Eat a wide variety of foods.

5. When I watch television:
   a. I have a routine of what programs I watch.
   b. I have no routine concerning programs.

6. My weekends:
   a. Rarely vary from week to week.
   b. Are filled with new activities.

7. I enjoy going to art museums and galleries:
   a. Rarely or never.
   b. Sometimes or always.

ARE YOU LOGICAL OR INTUITIVE? Give yourself one point for each time you circled **(A)**, and zero when you answered **(B)**. If you scored 4–7 points, you have left-brain dominance. You rely on logical solutions in your life. If you scored 3 points or fewer, you have right-brain dominance. You tend to be more intuitive, spontaneous, and visual.

ARE YOU ASSERTIVE ENOUGH?

It's essential to know when to assert yourself and when to be less up front with others on the job.

James G. Patterson, author of *How to Become a Better Negotiator* (AMACOM), maintains that you're appropriately assertive when you "stand up for your rights, are diplomatic, and have a 'win-win' problem-solving orientation." Using that definition as your criterion, respond to the following statements, based in part on a quiz in Patterson's book:

		YES	NO
1.	You express your opinion, even when someone in a senior position disagrees with you.	☐	☐
2.	You make direct eye contact when talking with others.	☐	☐
3.	You point out when someone's being unfair.	☐	☐
4.	Without apologizing, you say "No" to unreasonable demands.	☐	☐
5.	You recommend new ways of doing things on the job.	☐	☐
6.	You take the initiative to end phone calls when you're busy.	☐	☐
7.	You have confidence in your own judgment.	☐	☐
8.	When you meet someone for the first time, you introduce yourself and extend your hand.	☐	☐
9.	You offer your ideas and express your opinions rather than keep them to yourself.	☐	☐
10.	In a conflict, you're less concerned with "winning" than with reaching a mutually satisfying agreement.	☐	☐

TOTAL NUMBER OF YES ANSWERS _____

DO YOU STAND UP FOR YOURSELF? Consider yourself appropriately assertive if you responded **YES** to seven or more of the above statements. *A word of caution*: Many people confuse being assertive with being aggressive. Assertiveness doesn't mean defending your own rights at the expense of everyone else's. It also doesn't mean saying what you think to the point of brutal honesty. However, being assertive does entail taking responsibility for your interactions with others.

WHAT DRIVES YOUR COMPETITIVENESS?

People who are extremely competitive have long been considered "Type A" personalities. Experts consider Type A's to be a possible danger to themselves and others because of the pressure-cooker atmosphere they foster at work, particularly if their competitiveness includes the "potential for hostility," say William Lundin, Ph.D., and Kathleen Lundin, co-authors of *Working with Difficult People* (AMACOM).

Take the following quiz, based on an exercise in the Lundins' book. Respond **YES** or **NO** to each statement:

		YES	NO
1.	I need a challenge in order to feel fully alive.	☐	☐
2.	People have told me they consider me aggressive.	☐	☐
3.	When I feel strongly about something, I believe in getting it off my chest.	☐	☐
4.	People have said they sometimes find me intimidating.	☐	☐
5.	I'm a very impatient person when people don't do things right or meet my expectations.	☐	☐
6.	I believe winning is the most important thing of all.	☐	☐
7.	I tend to feel angry and resentful when someone else gets praise or honors I think I deserve.	☐	☐
8.	I really enjoy confrontations — people may get upset, but it livens things up.	☐	☐
9.	Other people have always had high expectations of me — and I show them I can meet those expectations.	☐	☐
10.	I have tremendous energy, and I put much of it into competing.	☐	☐
11.	I feel most competitive when I know my boss doesn't think I can handle something.	☐	☐
12.	I really enjoy competing when it involves beating someone else out or proving I'm better than they are.	☐	☐

HOW DO YOU VIEW COMPETITION? If you've responded **YES** to more than half of these statements, it would appear that hostility often drives your competitive impulses. It might be a good idea to explore the reasons why. Try to take a more cooperative approach.

WHO'S RIGHT ON GENDER DIFFERENCES?

According to Ruth Siress, author of *Working Woman's Communications Survival Guide* (Prentice Hall), men and women have fundamentally different styles of viewing and acting in the world.

To test your awareness of gender differences, take the following quiz, based on material in Siress' book. When answering, use this code:

A = USUALLY APPLIES TO WOMEN; B = USUALLY APPLIES TO MEN:

1. More oriented toward relationships, sharing, and cooperation. _____

2. Keenly interested in results, power, competition, and efficiency. _____

3. When entering a room, sits before observing the environment. _____

4. When entering a room, sits after observing the environment. _____

5. Prefers to talk on the telephone without interruption from anyone else in the room. _____

6. Easily handles multiple tasks, such as talking on the telephone, taking notes, and finding documents. _____

7. Likely to be overly responsible, overwhelmed, and frustrated by the needs of others. _____

8. Becomes absorbed by one problem at a time and is motivated by the most urgent problem of the moment. _____

9. Problem-solves by developing a plan of action. _____

10. More inclined to talk out problems. _____

THE ANSWERS: 1. A; 2. B; 3. B; 4. A; 5. B; 6. A; 7. A; 8. B; 9. B; 10. A

WHAT'S YOUR LEVEL OF GENDER AWARENESS? If you scored nine or 10 correct answers, you're aware of some of the basic tendencies of each gender, Siress says. If you had seven or eight correct answers, you may occasionally be "confused by the fundamental differences between men and women." Siress recommends studying gender issues and differences, and developing "respect for each gender's unique qualities."

ETHICS: ARE YOU COMMITTED?

Many companies today publish an ethical code of behavior for their employees and managers to follow. The specifics vary, but what ethics comes down to is: "To thine own self be true."

Take this quiz to gauge how ethical your own behavior is:

		YES	NO
1.	You have read your company's ethics guidelines and follow them closely.	☐	☐
2.	If an ethical situation is not covered specifically in the guidelines, you use your conscience as a guide.	☐	☐
3.	You're committed to doing the right thing, even when no one would know the difference.	☐	☐
4.	You believe it's wrong to "steal time" by arriving late or leaving early.	☐	☐
5.	"Everyone does it" is not an excuse for unethical behavior.	☐	☐
6.	You consider it important not to cheat in even small ways, such as taking office supplies home.	☐	☐
7.	You think even minor "fudging" on expenses is wrong.	☐	☐
8.	If you considered your boss' behavior unethical, you would let him or her know, rather than just "go along."	☐	☐
9.	You show respect for co-workers through your honesty, truthfulness, and reliability.	☐	☐
10.	You believe in always giving customers the value they're paying for.	☐	☐
11.	When you are wrong or make mistakes, you admit it and accept responsibility.	☐	☐
12.	You try to demonstrate ethical behavior.	☐	☐

TOTAL NUMBER OF YES ANSWERS _____

HOW ETHICAL ARE YOU? If you responded **YES** to nine or more of the above statements, you're strongly committed to acting ethically on the job. If you responded **YES** to fewer than eight, review all of the statements to get a stronger sense of what ethical behavior really involves.

DO YOU HAVE TROUBLE SPEAKING UP?

Do you need a boost in self-confidence? Take the following quiz to see if a simple lack of faith in yourself might be the problem when it comes to speaking up:

		Yes	No
1.	Do you feel successful on the job?	☐	☐
2.	Do you feel successful in your life?	☐	☐
3.	Under pressure, do you feel that things will work out?	☐	☐
4.	If a co-worker disagrees with you, do you see it as a simple difference of opinion that doesn't reflect on you?	☐	☐
5.	Do you solve many of the problems in your department?	☐	☐
6.	Do you take risks?	☐	☐
7.	Do you get a full night's sleep free of worry about work?	☐	☐
8.	Do your friends make you feel good about yourself?	☐	☐
9.	At meetings are you more concerned about issues than about what impressions you will make?	☐	☐
10.	In adversity, do you hold on to positive emotions?	☐	☐
11.	Most mornings, do you spring out of bed, looking forward to the challenges ahead of you?	☐	☐
12.	Do you often feel there isn't enough time in the day to accomplish everything you'd like?	☐	☐
13.	Do you set goals and constantly work to achieve them?	☐	☐

TOTAL NUMBER OF YES ANSWERS _____

WHAT'S YOUR CONFIDENCE QUOTIENT? Twelve to 13 **YES** answers indicate that you have a healthy level of self-confidence. Eight to 10 **YES** answers indicate a moderate level of self-confidence. You, at times, may not feel quite certain if your actions are going to produce the results you hope for. Seven or fewer **YES** answers indicate that you need to build your self-confidence. Spend some time each day focusing on your personal and professional successes.

DO YOU FEEL DISENCHANTED?

Even the best employees have days when it's a challenge to have that "up feeling." For most people, a mild form of depression usually goes away in a short time. But some people can feel dejection much longer. Below are six categories related to depression. Rate yourself on how you feel at this very moment:

1. PESSIMISM
(a) I look forward to the opportunities the future holds.
(b) I feel somewhat discouraged about the future.
(c) I feel the future is hopeless, and things won't get better.

2. SATISFACTION
(a) I'm very satisfied with my life.
(b) I don't enjoy things the way I once did.
(c) I'm really unhappy with most aspects of my life.

3. SOCIAL CONTACT
(a) I genuinely enjoy meeting and learning about people.
(b) I find myself losing interest in what others have to say.
(c) I avoid situations where I have to meet new people.

4. SELF-ESTEEM
(a) I approve of who I am.
(b) I'm somewhat disappointed in myself.
(c) I hate myself.

5. INSOMNIA
(a) I sleep as well as I ever could.
(b) I wake up more tired in the mornings than I used to.
(c) It's rare that I sleep soundly through the night.

6. WORK
(a) The quality and quantity of my work remains high.
(b) I don't work as well as I used to.
(c) I really have to push myself to get my work done.

SCORING: Give yourself three points for each (a) answer, two points for each (b) answer, and one point for each (c) answer. **HIGH: 18 POINTS.** You feel good about yourself and your life. **MEDIUM: 14–17 POINTS.** You have an upbeat outlook, although you may find it a challenge to get through certain days. **LOW: 13 POINTS OR FEWER.** A self-help program should give you a new perspective in handling your depression.

WHEN DOES ANGER PUT US AT RISK?

Letting anger routinely "get the better of you" can make for unpleasant and unproductive working relationships. It also can pose a potential safety risk to others — and a stress-related health risk to you! So it would be a good idea to explore what part anger plays in your work life. Take the following quiz, responding **YES** or **NO** to each statement:

		YES	NO
1.	You feel angry often — either every day or several times a week.	☐	☐
2.	You frequently find yourself expressing anger at others.	☐	☐
3.	Even when you don't want to express anger, you find yourself doing so anyway.	☐	☐
4.	You often end up apologizing to co-workers or supervisors for your outbursts.	☐	☐
5.	You get upset when your performance is less than perfect.	☐	☐
6.	You get mad at others when they make even minor mistakes.	☐	☐
7.	People at work have commented more than once on your tendency to get angry.	☐	☐
8.	When angry, you have physically harmed another person.	☐	☐
9.	You look for ways to "get" people whom you feel have insulted you or let you down.	☐	☐
10.	In the heat of anger, you have thrown or broken things.	☐	☐

DO YOU HAVE AN ANGER PROBLEM? That could be the case if you responded **YES** to more than three of the above statements. It might be helpful to begin "destressing" yourself so that feelings of anger don't hold such power over you. Take daily quiet times to decompress. Learn how to meditate, for instance, or listen to peaceful music. When you start feeling stressed or angry, do a brief visualization — imagining yourself becoming calm in a relaxing situation. Also consider turning to someone you trust, such as a good friend or spiritual adviser, for comfort and guidance.

IS YOUR MOUTH FASTER THAN E-MAIL?

Do you have a tendency to gossip? Are you not always discreet with private information? Do people get the impression that you have loose lips? Answer the following questions to help shed some light:

		YES	NO
1.	Do you engage in nonproductive discussions about colleagues and work issues several times a day?	☐	☐
2.	Do you feel the need to blow off steam by ranting about a difficult colleague?	☐	☐
3.	Do you feel a "rush" of energy when you share information that a confidant didn't know?	☐	☐
4.	Do you assume that, if someone doesn't want you to share information, he or she will tell you directly?	☐	☐
5.	Do you rely more on the office grapevine for work information than you do on formal communication?	☐	☐
6.	Do you have trouble keeping a secret even when asked to?	☐	☐
7.	Do colleagues — even those with whom you are close — rarely come to you with personal issues?	☐	☐
8.	Do you feel you have a right to know "what's going on," even if it has nothing to do with you or your job?	☐	☐

TOTAL NUMBER OF YES ANSWERS _____

ARE YOU A GOSSIP? Each **YES** answer to these questions is a sign of an office gossip. If you have six or more **YES** answers, you may want to review your behavior at work. Realize that there is a difference between information sharing and gossip. The former involves keeping lines of communication open so that important information — information necessary for doing your job — gets to all employees who need it. Gossiping is rarely productive and more often destructive. If you want to avoid the title of office gossip, you'll have to show that it's not warranted. Take one situation at a time and keep your mouth shut.

DOES OPINION MATTER TOO MUCH TO YOU?

Some people find it impossible to have self-esteem unless they get praise from others. As a result, they sacrifice their credibility and integrity by being obsessed with approval. Are you addicted to approval from others? Take the following quiz to find out:

		YES	NO
1.	Do you take criticism personally?	☐	☐
2.	Do you give up your interests to please your boss and co-workers?	☐	☐
3.	Do you solicit co-workers for compliments?	☐	☐
4.	Do you do what other people want just so they won't be angry with you?	☐	☐
5.	Does your value as a person depend mostly upon what others say about you?	☐	☐
6.	Is it important that acquaintances instantly like you, even if you don't like them?	☐	☐
7.	If someone rejects your idea, do you automatically blame your inadequacies?	☐	☐
8.	Do you always fear something will go wrong on a project — and that it will be your fault?	☐	☐
9.	Do you berate yourself when you make a mistake?	☐	☐
10.	If you disagree with someone, do you always apologize first and accept all the blame?	☐	☐

TOTAL NUMBER OF YES ANSWERS _____

HOW MUCH DOES YOUR PUBLIC MATTER? A score of eight or more **YES** answers suggests that other people's opinions matter more to you than your self-perceptions. That could very well prevent you from taking risks that could advance you personally and professionally. Six or seven **YES** answers indicate that you should have a higher opinion of yourself. A lower score suggests that outside opinion doesn't usually shake your sense of self-worth.

MAKE WORK MORE INTERESTING

While it may be difficult to find every aspect of your work exciting, you cannot afford to let boredom interfere with your career if you wish to be successful. So what are some effective ways to make your work more interesting? The following quiz will not only offer you some ideas, but will also test your capacity for doing so. Evaluate your efforts by answering **YES** or **NO** to each question:

		YES	NO
1.	Do you leave "boring" tasks for periods of the day when your energy level is usually low?	☐	☐
2.	Do you dive into your work first thing in the morning?	☐	☐
3.	Do you spice up your work by occasionally changing your routine?	☐	☐
4.	Do you experiment with new approaches to your work?	☐	☐
5.	Do you ask others for ways to make your work more interesting?	☐	☐
6.	Do you look for new and interesting discoveries in your work?	☐	☐
7.	When you complete a tedious task, do you reward yourself — for example, by following it with a job you really enjoy?	☐	☐
8.	Do you focus more intently on the objective of your work rather than on the process itself?	☐	☐
9.	Do you remind yourself about the potential rewards and benefits of doing a good job?	☐	☐
10.	Do you try to work with different co-workers to expose yourself to a variety of perspectives?	☐	☐

ARE YOU INTERESTED? If you answered **YES** to each of the above questions, then you are probably very successful in making your job as interesting as possible. If not, then you will need to commit to putting forth some effort in this area. Remember, the more interesting you can make your work, the more enjoyable it will become. It's a cycle that, once started, will be hard to break.

MAKING TIME FOR YOURSELF

Balancing work and family means making time for yourself. But people often feel guilty for "indulging" in time for themselves. How can you determine whether you've found the right mix between handling your outside responsibilities and taking care of yourself?

Take the following quiz, based on a "self-nurturing evaluation" designed by The Center for Work and the Family, to determine your ability to balance work and your personal life.

Rate yourself on a scale of **1** through **5**. As a general guideline, give yourself a **1** for "I have difficulty taking care of myself this way," **3** for "Fair," and **5** for "I care for myself well in this way":

1. You eat a healthy diet, staying away from junk foods and too much caffeine and alcohol. _____

2. You follow a regular (but not rigid) exercise plan. _____

3. You get the amount of sleep you need in order to feel alert and energetic during the day. _____

4. You arrange to spend some time alone on a regular basis. _____

5. You spend time regularly with your partner. _____

6. You spend time regularly with family members and/or friends. _____

7. You allow yourself "play time"—for recreation, hobbies, or sports, for instance. _____

8. You tend to your spiritual needs in whatever way is important to you. _____

9. You set realistic expectations for yourself. _____

10. You tend to your personal growth—by developing certain talents, when possible, or exploring subjects of particular interest to you. _____

YOUR SELF-CARE QUOTIENT is high if you gave yourself at least eight **5** ratings. You've found a healthy balance. If your score is lower, review the statements in this quiz. Look for clues as to how you can take better care of yourself as you go about meeting your work and family commitments.

Note: The Center for Work and the Family offers programs and training in work/family integration. For information, contact the center at 910 Tulare Ave., Berkeley, CA 94707; (510) 527-0107.

CREATING THAT 'PROFESSIONAL' IMAGE

If you want to be regarded as a professional, you must look and act like one. Why? When you present yourself as a polished professional, others will accept you on those terms — as long as your performance is equally professional.

Take the following quiz to determine the quality of your current professional image:

	YES	NO
1. Do you know someone who has the professional image you would like to develop?	☐	☐
2. Have you analyzed how your role model creates that image?	☐	☐
3. Do you pay scrupulous attention to your personal hygiene?	☐	☐
4. Does your hairstyle suit your face and convey a professional look?	☐	☐
5. Do you plan your wardrobe carefully?	☐	☐
6. Do your posture and gestures convey the image of a confident professional?	☐	☐
7. Do you follow a regular exercise regimen to keep yourself healthy and fit?	☐	☐
8. Is your attitude positive and your image upbeat and motivated?	☐	☐
9. Do you follow proper etiquette?	☐	☐
10. Do your voice and diction sound professional?	☐	☐
11. Do you treat other people with respect, kindness, and honesty?	☐	☐

TOTAL NUMBER OF YES ANSWERS   _____

HOW IS YOUR IMAGE? If you've answered **YES** to nine or more of these questions, you're well on your way to a professional image that will contribute to your success. If you've answered **YES** to fewer than nine questions, think about how you can improve the way you look, act, and speak to convey your professionalism.

MEASURING UP:
LEAD THE WAY IN CREATIVITY

You can encourage creativity by example. When you approach everyday problems and concerns creatively, your more perceptive co-workers will likely notice and follow suit. To learn more about encouraging their creativity, take the following quiz. Answer each question with **YES** or **NO**:

	YES	NO
1. Do you let others identify problems rather than jumping in too quickly with your own views?	☐	☐
2. Do you encourage people to challenge the way things have always been done in the past?	☐	☐
3. Do you support the "free flow" of ideas rather than cut off the brainstorming too soon?	☐	☐
4. Are you willing to entertain "far out" solutions as a way of breaking free of established thinking patterns?	☐	☐
5. Do you listen without interrupting or judging when others are expressing their ideas?	☐	☐
6. Do you tolerate ambiguity, accepting that often there's no "right" or "wrong" answer, only differing perspectives?	☐	☐
7. Are you flexible enough to change your mind when the evidence strongly supports another viewpoint?	☐	☐
8. Do you avoid putting others' ideas down, even when you think those ideas are totally unworkable?	☐	☐
9. Do you good-naturedly accept consensus decisions even when you don't agree with them?	☐	☐
10. Are you willing to take a calculated risk even though you can't be sure how things will turn out?	☐	☐

TOTAL NUMBER OF YES ANSWERS _____

DO YOU NURTURE CREATIVITY? A score of at least nine **YES** answers indicates that your creative approach to your daily job is probably a good example. If you scored fewer than nine **YES** answers, you might want to reconsider what creativity support involves.

ARE YOU MINDING YOUR MANNERS?

Courtesy counts in each and every encounter you have with people. It "oils the wheels of commerce" by maintaining harmony among coworkers and with customers. Answer the following questions **YES** or **NO**:

		YES	NO
1.	Is there a "most courteous person" you admire?	☐	☐
2.	Do you see it as your job to serve everyone with whom you come into contact — boss, colleague, and customer?	☐	☐
3.	Is it your attitude that "nothing is too much trouble if it means people are satisfied with the help they receive"?	☐	☐
4.	Are you aware when you're having "bad mood" days, so that you can take extra precautions to stay cool, calm, and polite?	☐	☐
5.	Do you always acknowledge — with a smile and a greeting — the people who walk up to your desk?	☐	☐
6.	Do you identify yourself by name to callers when you answer the telephone and to the person on the other end of the line when you make a call?	☐	☐
7.	Do you make it a matter of routine to say "Please" and "Thank you"?	☐	☐
8.	Do you consider good manners the essence of good business — and prove it through consistently positive interactions with others?	☐	☐
9.	Do you avoid potentially offensive behaviors, such as the use of profanity, telling off-color jokes, and using first names when you meet people?	☐	☐
10.	Are you in the habit of asking people "How do you pronounce your name?" when necessary?	☐	☐

TOTAL NUMBER OF YES ANSWERS _____

WHAT'S YOUR COURTESY QUOTIENT? If you answered **YES** to eight or more questions, you're likely putting your best manners forward on the job. If you answered **YES** to fewer than eight, review the contents of this quiz to see how you can improve your etiquette.

CULTIVATE YOUR CHARISMA

Charisma is personal confidence, as opposed to job confidence. Charismatic people exude confidence, strength, and leadership. Take the following quiz to rate your charisma:

	Yes	No
1. When speaking to others, you are in control of your speech rate, and where and how you move.	☐	☐
2. Others perceive you as strong, calm, and motivational.	☐	☐
3. You know exactly when and how to interject your opinions.	☐	☐
4. You convey your thoughts and show your feelings with conviction.	☐	☐
5. You have an appropriate sense of humor.	☐	☐
6. You take risks and can get others to believe in you and join you.	☐	☐
7. You have concrete goals and a sense of purpose.	☐	☐
8. When you move, you move with certainty.	☐	☐
9. You take an interest in what others have to say and do not dominate conversations.	☐	☐
10. You are not overly concerned with what others think of you.	☐	☐
11. You know how to control an audience and keep its attention.	☐	☐

TOTAL NUMBER OF YES ANSWERS   _____

HOW CHARISMATIC ARE YOU? A highly charismatic person would have answered **YES** to all of the above statements. If you answered **YES** to more than seven statements, you have some charisma. You know how to get people to stop and take notice, but you waiver in confidence at times. If you answered **YES** to fewer than seven statements, you are lacking a very important part of communication and presentation.

Analyze the statements to which you answered **NO**. These are the areas you need to work on to increase your charisma.

A POSITIVE OUTLOOK IMPROVES ANY DAY

A positive outlook can ease us through even the bleakest of days. And it can make it easier to get along with even the most difficult co-worker. We all control whether we choose to be positive or negative. Which do you choose to be? Take the following quiz to find out. Respond **YES** to the statements that apply to you:

		YES	NO
1.	I truly believe that I am a valuable and worthwhile person.	☐	☐
2.	I recognize and capitalize on my personal strengths.	☐	☐
3.	I accept my weaknesses and change whatever I can.	☐	☐
4.	I can find the humor in life — even if it makes me look a little ridiculous at times.	☐	☐
5.	I look for new experiences and enjoy the surprises life presents along the way.	☐	☐
6.	I enjoy meeting new people and learning about who they are and what they think and do.	☐	☐
7.	I appreciate those people who are different from me.	☐	☐
8.	Generally, I don't worry about what I cannot control.	☐	☐
9.	I don't get bogged down by difficulties and setbacks.	☐	☐
10.	I accept responsibility for my mistakes and try to learn from them.	☐	☐

TOTAL NUMBER OF YES ANSWERS _____

HOW POSITIVE ARE YOU? If you scored eight or more **YES** answers, congratulations. You walk on "the sunny side of the street." But, then, we probably don't have to tell you that. It's likely, too, that you do your share to brighten others' days at the same time.

If you didn't tally many **YES** answers, try experimenting with one or two of those **NO** answers — make them into **YES** ones for a day or two. Chances are, you'll find that you will get more done, and you'll feel better at the end of the day. And that feeling can be nothing short of addictive.

WHAT'S YOUR PERSONAL LONG SUIT?

Many career experts claim that the key to success is the ability to maximize personal strengths while minimizing weaknesses. But, sometimes it's not easy to know exactly what those strengths are. Do you know what you excel at — abilities that can contribute to your success? Take the following quiz to find out. When considering a specific skill or ability:

		YES	NO
1.	Does it feel like it's second nature to you, as if you've always known how to do it?	☐	☐
2.	Do you enjoy using this particular attribute?	☐	☐
3.	Do you like applying this ability, even if you're not getting paid for it?	☐	☐
4.	Is this ability something you do well, maybe even better, than most?	☐	☐
5.	Do others recognize this ability, even if you're not getting paid for it?	☐	☐
6.	Do you find yourself practicing it on your own, just to refine it even further?	☐	☐
7.	Do you think you could make money applying this skill or ability?	☐	☐
8.	Would it be possible to complement this ability with another one of your skills?	☐	☐
9.	Is it occasionally a source of pride for you?	☐	☐
10.	Has this ability been mentioned on previous performance reviews?	☐	☐

TOTAL NUMBER OF YES ANSWERS _____

YOUR SCORE: A score of eight or more **YES** answers suggests that this particular ability could be your ticket to success. Even a score of five or more means that this skill has potential — it just might need nurturing by you. This requires patience and a little courage. It's not always easy admitting what we excel at. But it's essential to know what strengths we can build upon.

WHAT'S YOUR LIFETIME PLAN?

The following test was compiled by James R. Sherman, Ph.D., author of *Plan Your Work: Work Your Plan* (Crisp Publications). As you take the test, be honest with yourself about where you are and what you want to do:

1. What are the most significant events that have taken place in your life in the last three to five years? Why do you think they're important? _____

    _____

    _____

2. What's your record of successes and failures? _____

    _____

3. What's your position in the world today? _____

    _____

4. How well are you performing? _____

    _____

5. What have you accomplished?_____

    _____

    _____

6. How high do you want to go on the ladder of success? _____

    _____

7. What are your three most important life goals?_____

    _____

8. What's your philosophy of life? _____

    _____

9. How are you going to get where you want to go?_____

    _____

10. How will you know when you've completed the milestones that you've identified? _____

    _____

YOUR FUTURE: There are no right or wrong answers here, but you can quickly determine if the lifestyle course that you've chosen is right for you. Put this test aside, and make an appointment to evaluate yourself a year from now to assess your progress.

RESOURCE GUIDE

THE VALUE OF REINFORCED TRAINING

Take This Quiz to Test Your Knowledge of Current Training Trends:

1. What percentage of information that employees need to do their jobs is acquired through formal training?
   ❑ 38 percent   ❑ 68 percent   ❑ 88 percent

2. What is the most frequently used training method?
   ❑ Public seminars   ❑ Classroom programs
   ❑ Computer-based training

3. What percentage of training do your employees actually retain?
   ❑ 60 percent   ❑ 25 percent   ❑ 15 percent

Answers:

1. Only **38 percent** of the knowledge employees need to do their jobs is acquired through formal training programs, according to the Teaching Firm Research Report. It is mostly through informal learning — participation in teams, meetings, customer interactions, talking with supervisors, mentoring, and peer-to-peer communication that employees learn the skills they need, the report reveals.

2. The vast majority of organizations, 94 percent, still use **live instructors in a classroom setting**, but 77 percent of all training — be it in a classroom setting or not — incorporates the **use of printed materials**, reveals Industry Report 1997.

3. Without reinforcement, people retain as little as **15 percent** of what they learned during training after only 3 days, says Dr. Barbara Carnes, president of Carnes and Associates, Inc., a St. Louis-based human resources development and consulting firm. What they actually use is even less, she says.

How do you maximize informal training, enhance classroom training, and convert that discouraging 15 percent retention rate into an 80 percent rate of positive behavioral change?

By providing your employees with continuous, reinforced training through **Dartnell newsletters** and other publications such as **Quick Quizzes: 133 Ways to Measure Success** and the interactive **Dartnell High-Performance Skill Builder workbook series**.

DARTNELL NEWSLETTERS

A **Dartnell newsletter's** delivery schedule gives employees a consistent flow of information to reinforce your other company training programs. The "quick read" and self-directed nature of the material encourages readers to apply what they learn to their individual work situations. The newsletter can dramatically improve the return on your training investment by helping trainees recall and apply productivity-boosting concepts and techniques.

Dartnell has a newsletter for each member of your organization covering topics including **teamwork, customer service, supervisory skills, selling, communication,** and **telephone skills**.

FREE ISSUE NEWSLETTER CLAIM FORM

YES! Send me two free issues of the following **Dartnell newsletters**!

	No. of Copies		No. of Copies
TEAMWORK		*CUSTOMERS FIRST*	_____
MANUFACTURING EDITION	_____	*INBOUND SERVICE*	_____
OFFICE EDITION	_____	*EFFECTIVE TELEPHONE*	
TEAM LEADER	_____	*TECHNIQUES*	_____
WORKING TOGETHER	_____	*OUTBOUND SELLING*	_____
FIRST LINE SUPERVISOR	_____	*SALESMANSHIP*	_____
SUCCESSFUL SUPERVISOR	_____	*OVERCOMING OBJECTIONS*	_____
FROM 9 TO 5	_____	*SUCCESSFUL CLOSING*	
GETTING ALONG	_____	*TECHNIQUES*	_____
COMMUNICATION AT WORK	_____	*NEW ACCOUNT SELLING*	_____
QUALITY 1ST	_____		

If I like what I see, I'll approve your invoice based on the prices shown below, plus postage and handling, and continue to receive issues of my chosen newsletter(s) every two weeks for a full year. If I decide not to subscribe, I'll simply write "Cancel" on the invoice, return it, and owe nothing. All of the free issues are mine to keep in any case.

Pricing:

    5 to 9 copies ....$1.79 each copy
    10 to 49 copies ....$1.69 each copy
    50 to 99 copies ....$1.65 each copy

Name_____

Signature _____

Company _____

Address _____

City/State/ZIP _____

Phone (   ) _____Fax (   ) _____

DARTNELL'S HIGH-PERFORMANCE SKILL BUILDER WORKBOOKS

Each workbook in Dartnell's High-Performance Skill Builder series contains five sessions of short bursts of training. Each workbook in this popular, effective series provides how-to information for a specific job function or skill in a quick and easy self-study format. By devoting only 20 minutes each day for one week, you and your employees will learn and retain new skills that can be put to work on the job immediately.

Every session includes skill assessment quizzes so that progress can be measured. The workbooks use a variety of interesting and entertaining learning methods, such as case studies, personal productivity exercises, and customized action plans. Covering the key business topics of **Sales, Customer Service,** and **Teamwork**, this performance-building series is an excellent training program in itself or a fine complement and reinforcement for other training you or your employees might receive.